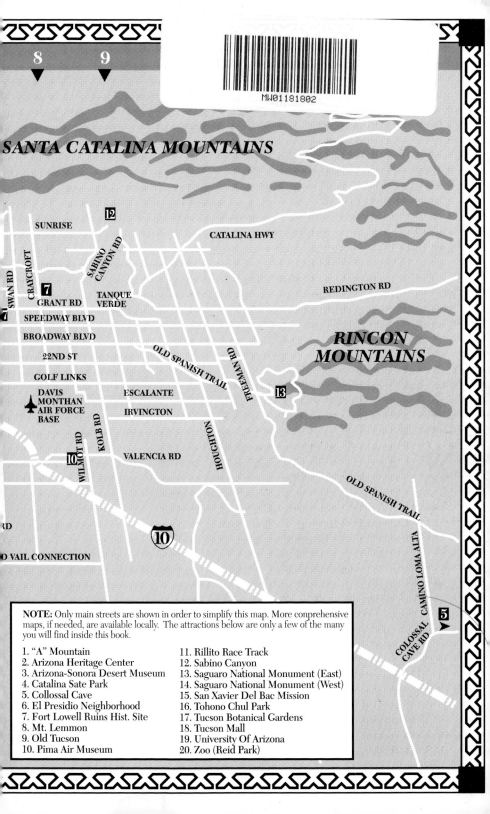

8 ▼ **9** ▼

MW01181802

SANTA CATALINA MOUNTAINS

SUNRISE 12

CATALINA HWY

SABINO CANYON RD

SWAN RD

CRAYCROFT

7 GRANT RD TANQUE VERDE

REDINGTON RD

7 SPEEDWAY BLVD

BROADWAY BLVD

RINCON MOUNTAINS

22ND ST

OLD SPANISH TRAIL

FREEMAN RD

GOLF LINKS

DAVIS MONTHAN AIR FORCE BASE ESCALANTE

IRVINGTON 13

KOLB RD

WILMOT RD

HOUGHTON

10 VALENCIA RD

OLD SPANISH TRAIL

RD

10

VAIL CONNECTION

COLOSSAL CAVE RD CAMINO LOMA ALTA

5 ▶

NOTE: Only main streets are shown in order to simplify this map. More conprehensive maps, if needed, are available locally. The attractions below are only a few of the many you will find inside this book.

1. "A" Mountain
2. Arizona Heritage Center
3. Arizona-Sonora Desert Museum
4. Catalina Sate Park
5. Collossal Cave
6. El Presidio Neighborhood
7. Fort Lowell Ruins Hist. Site
8. Mt. Lemmon
9. Old Tucson
10. Pima Air Museum

11. Rillito Race Track
12. Sabino Canyon
13. Saguaro National Monument (East)
14. Saguaro National Monument (West)
15. San Xavier Del Bac Mission
16. Tohono Chul Park
17. Tucson Botanical Gardens
18. Tucson Mall
19. University Of Arizona
20. Zoo (Reid Park)

SCENIC TUCSON
A Guide To Seeing The Best Of The Tucson Area
by
Bob Kerry

Drawings by Terri Gay
Production, Design, Maps by Mike McPherson
Photos not otherwise credited, ©Bob Kerry

Copyright 1994
Backcountry Books of Arizona LLC
3390 N. Campbell Ave. Suite 120
Tucson, Arizona 85719
Phone 602-325-8150
Fax 325-4208

Other than for the purposes of a review in a publication of general circulation, no part of this book or any illustration, photograph or map contained in it may be reproduced by any means without the written permission of Backcountry Books of Arizona LLC.

Changes or Corrections
The author would appreciate hearing about any changes or corrections. Please address them to Backcountry Books at the above address.

Library of Congress Catalog Card Number 93-73902

Cover Photo: Mission San Xavier del Bac, ©David Muench Photography

Acknowledgments

This guide is a homegrown Tucson product. It draws on the efforts of many people and it was a pleasure to find such a talented group of Tucsonans to supply the elements. The cover photo by David Muench is the only contribution by someone not from Tucson. But, since he is sort of the "godfather" of Southwestern scenic photography, he seems like a native to many Tucsonans.

My wife Lynn Kerry labored on research, writing, editing, map reading and provided a great deal of creative input. Terri Gay drew the illustrations, adding a touch sometimes whimsical, sometimes romantic. Mike McPherson provided the design and layout. He also drew the maps. The photographs which appear here are the work of several Tucson photographers, including the author. Editorial assistance by Roseann Hanson was invaluable. The staff at Arizona Lithographers was very helpful in packaging the entire ball of wax.

Kitt Peak

TABLE OF CONTENTS

MAP LIST

This guide contains **explicit directions** on how to see some of the best of Tucson's and Southern Arizona's unique scenery and events. Organized by area of interest, it is intended to help you get good views and photographs.

The idea for this guide was formulated standing in line in Tucson photo stores listening to visitors ask store clerks for information on where to go to take good photos of the sunset, cactus, birds or whatever. The clerks did the best they could to help, considering they were waiting on other customers. The visitors hastily scribbled directions and went on their way. Often it was clear they were going to have problems finding what they were looking for.

For 22 years I have driven, hiked and climbed over much of Southern Arizona. In this guide I've drawn together a collection of information that will help you see the best of the Tucson Area and Southern Arizona with a minimum of wasted time. Of course I can't guarantee that there will be a killer Arizona sunset just when you are ready, but I can tell you of a great place to get a view of the sunset, obstructed only by the saguaros or other cactus you chose to have in the foreground.

No guide to the scenic beauty of Tucson can hope to be exhaustive. The spectacular desert scenery and outstanding light may present a gem of a view at the most unexpected turn. This book only suggests some places to start. I hope in using this guide that you discover your own favorite Tucson places.

How To Use This Guide

Look over the **maps** inside the front and back covers and find where you are. Look over the **Calendar of Events** in Appendix One for things that interest you. **Scan the table of contents** to get an idea of what is covered. When organizing your outings you may be tempted to include as many locations as possible in each one. **Don't rush.** Limit your coverage so you can get the **best light** and have some time to sit and soak in the feel of the area. If you miss something, you will have that to look forward to next time.

I've assumed you have a car, so no directions are given for public transportation. Many of the areas covered are not served by public transportation anyway.

The entries for Tucson are identified by the area of town, and a specific reference to the **map** on the inside front cover. Also there are specific directions to most locations. In some cases there are additional maps to the area. Daytrips are referenced to the map of southern Arizona on the inside back cover.

Be sure to check this guide for times, both when the location is open and the best time for light. A chart showing **when the sun rises and sets** is included in Appendix Two.

If you have a **dog**, check the rules. There are a lot of places you can't take your friend. This may be a problem. In the hot weather you cannot leave your pet in the car for even a short period of time without risking cooking him or her in the intense desert heat. At the least, find a shady spot to tie your friend up and be sure to leave a water bowl that won't be tipped over.

Many restaurants are mentioned in passing, as are hotels and dude ranches. **The Tucson Official Visitors Guide** is indispensable for the latest up-to-date information on hotels, restaurants and shopping. It is available at the Metropolitan Tucson Convention & Visitors Bureau, 130 S. Scott Ave., Tucson, 85701, 602-624-1817. The Tucson Weekly newspaper is distributed free around town and has excellent coverage of cultural events, especially the "hipper ones".

Photo Tips

You don't have to be a photographer to use this book. If you are interested in taking your memories away in your heart instead of on film, that's fine. You can still benefit from these directions so you can enjoy the places you came to see instead of driving around lost.

Photographers of all skill and experience levels can use this book for information and directions. Throughout the guide there are general photo tips, some apply especially to the desert or the area being discussed. They will seem basic to experienced photographers but they may serve as reminders, and help anyone to go home with better pictures. Appendix Ten contains a list of basic photography do's and don'ts. Many of the tips apply to **video** as well as still photography. The glary light of midday can wreck a video shot as badly as it can wash out a still photo.

If you try something new, be sure to take another shot using methods you are sure will work so you are not disappointed if the experiment fails. You are better off sticking with what you know will work than experimenting with new techniques on vacation where you will not be able to reshoot mistakes. Nonetheless, certain basics, such as getting close enough to your subject, or scheduling to shoot in the best light, should help without the risk of such catastrophe.

About Relationships

Many people seem to stress out on vacation and not have a good time. One major reason is quarrels with the "significant other," the

Thunderstorm over Tucson, © Wm. L. Wantland

husband, wife, boyfriend or girlfriend. Often the reason is that one person has an idea of what is a good time that the other person doesn't share. Each is out to make sure they have their fair share of "fun" on this vacation and conflict ensues when they think they are being cheated out of their share.

Some of the outings in this guide involve walking and/or getting up at an early hour. If your mate would rather sleep in, play golf or mall cruise, let him or her do so, and enjoy the outing on your own. Live and let live, and you will both enjoy your vacation more.

The same goes for children. If they are young enough they will probably love these outings, but many teenagers are not "into nature" as my 14-year old daughter once informed me. Cut them some slack and let them enjoy the vacation too by visiting the water park or whatever they prefer once in awhile.

Safety

Without a doubt the biggest danger to you will be traffic. While rubbernecking around, please take the time to pull over to read maps and guides. Also, keep a close eye out for others who aren't watching where they are going. Be especially careful on the **Mount Lemmon Highway** which has a terrible accident record.

Lightning is a realistic danger around Tucson. If there is an approaching storm, stay in the car. Being on high places or in open areas where you are the highest point will put you in danger of being struck.

Rattlesnakes are an overrated danger. They are usually pretty docile and rattle only to let you know they are there and are worried. Leave them alone. Also, they seem to be attracted by alcohol; most victims have a high blood alcohol content. If you are bitten, there is conflicting advice on first aid, but there is agreement that the best thing is to get the victim to the hospital as soon as possible. I carry a venom extractor which is available at outdoor stores. There is debate over its effectiveness but it makes me feel better. Incidentally, I've jogged and walked over rattlers, stepped on them, danced on them in deep brush and even rolled over on one, but never have I been bitten. Worry about the traffic.

There are **scorpions** and such bugs around Tucson but if you watch where you put your hands you should be all right. Even if you are stung, most scorpion stings are pretty harmless. If you start to react go to the emergency room for treatment.

Be careful around the cliffs in the mountains and especially around waterfalls in the canyons. People do occasionally fall. A little common sense should keep you safe. Don't rockclimb without training and the right equipment. This may seem obvious but there are some folks who don't seem to understand gravity and what even a 10-foot fall can do to the human body. Also, the rocks around the waterfalls are very slippery and the falls are powerful. Twenty-seven people have died at **Tanque Verde Falls** since they started counting in 1971.

Weather

Charts of average temperature and rainfall are contained in Appendices Two and Three. The most important thing to know about the weather in Tucson is that the dry heat causes you to lose water a lot faster than you think. When hiking around be sure to drink a lot of water. If you don't, you may get a bad headache or even clinical dehydration or heat exhaustion which can be life-threatening.

Tucson is at about 2,600 feet above sea level. Mount Lemmon is at 9,157 feet. It is always going to be a lot cooler on the mountain. See Appendix Three to compare the average temperatures in town and on Mount Lemmon.

The most dramatic weather is the summer thunderstorms. Giant cumulonimbus clouds spring up out of nowhere to tower 30,000 feet over the mountains. They make great photos, but don't forget about the lightning.

It can actually snow in Tucson. When it does it's gorgeous, and you can hear the camera shutters clicking above the traffic noise. It snows a lot more often up on Mount Lemmon, and there are great photos and views

to be had when the road clears and dries off. When there is ice and snow on the road, exercise extreme caution. Chains or four wheel drive are often required if the road is snow-covered.

Be flexible. There are always good things to see and great photos to be taken even when the weather seems most uncooperative. The mountains can be very interesting when swathed in clouds. When all else fails the indoor attractions such as the Arizona State Museum, the Arizona Heritage Museum, the Flandrau Planetarium or the art and artifact collections at the Amerind Foundation are worth exploring.

T he most widely recognized symbol of Arizona is the sunset. It's on the state flag and on running shorts, tee shirts, bolo ties and just about everywhere else you look in Arizona. But all these human attempts to graphically illustrate the sunset fail utterly to capture the thrilling beauty of the real thing. You cannot help being awed by the spectacle of the vast Arizona sky being painted from horizon to horizon with technicolor hues that haven't even been invented until the instant they appear.

Great sunsets can come at any time of year, but they need clouds. Oh, the afterglow in the western sky, which appears for months after a volcano has blown up somewhere, is impressive but it lacks the range of color which makes a truly memorable sunset. The summer thunderstorms produce towering cumulus clouds which light up wonderfully at sunset, both in the west and the east. The most spectacular sunsets often come in winter, when long banks of stratus clouds hang around after a Pacific storm has lumbered through the southwest. Sunset times are in Appendix Two.

Naturally you can see such a sunset from anywhere in **Tucson**, so why do you need directions? Well, you don't unless you'd like to enjoy the ceremony alone or at least from a quiet place in the desert, perhaps with cactus wrens providing the background music. Also if you are interested in taking a memorable photo, it helps to be where you can fit a nice big saguaro in the foreground for effect, or at least not have to include telephone poles in the scene.

Of the five areas discussed in this section, **Gates Pass** is the most well known and is likely to be a little crowded. Nonetheless, if you walk a little ways you'll probably find a nice quiet place. **Saguaro National Monument (West)** provides more flexibility in the foreground with lots of saguaros. It will be less crowded than Gates Pass and a lot quieter.

Catalina State Park has a host of scenic offerings but the real attraction here is the view of the **Santa Catalina Mountains** catching the late afternoon sun. Especially spectacular are the huge granite domes at the head of Alamo Canyon. The big triangular one is called Leviathan and right behind it is Wilderness Dome.

Pontatoc Ridge is closest to town and the resort hotels.

On the east side, **Saguaro National Monument (East)** presents an unobstructed view across the Tucson Valley and has the bonus of a view of the Santa Catalina Mountains in the sunset.

Facing Page: Saguaros at sunset, Sabino Canyon

Sunset

Windy Point is different from the other locations because it sits at 6,000 feet in the Santa Catalina Mountains. Like Gates Pass it can be noisy, but it is still highly recommended because of the dramatic clifftop situation and the expansive view of the entire valley with the city lights blinking on.

Photo tips. The low light of the sunset means you are going to use a low shutter speed, whether you select it or your automatic camera does. To avoid a blurry picture, use a **tripod** or brace the camera on something and hope for the best. A trick that will sometimes work to get a clear picture in these circumstances is to set the camera on a surface and set the **self timer** if it has one. Since you are not touching the camera when it makes the exposure, there is a good chance it will be steady enough to get a clear picture.

Don't overlook your **flash** at sunset time, a stunning photo can result when a subject is photographed against the sunset with enough fill flash to properly expose the subject. Give it a try, many modern cameras will do a good job automatically.

Don't give up too early. Often the best light comes long after the sun sets. But, when stomping around the desert taking these really great pictures, don't forget to take a flashlight if you are getting back to the car after dark. The terrain is rugged out there and rattlesnakes become pretty active at this time of day in the warmer weather. On the other hand, you are very unlikely to see a rattler in the cooler weather (mid-November to mid-March or so).

Look behind you. Sometimes the prettiest and most subtle colors will appear in the eastern sky as it is lit up. This is especially true in the summer when there are big thunderheads to catch the light. Also, the mountains will sometimes radiate a beautiful glow from the sunset if you have the right angle on them.

GATES PASS

Area of Town: West Side.

Map Reference: E 3.

Phone Number: 602-740-2690 (Pima County Parks & Recreation)

Directions: Take Speedway Blvd. west past I-10. It turns into a smaller winding road up into the mountains and changes names to Gates Pass Road. Follow it up to the pass where the road cuts sharply left and heads down. Here you make a sharp right into the parking lot. Once you park there are a number of tracks which lead up to viewpoints on the hillsides. One of my favorites is to go back across the road and follow the vague trail up the hill and choose one of the excellent viewpoints there. You really can't go wrong unless you happen to choose a spot that attracts a loud group.

Best Time of Year: All year.

Best Time of Day: Sunset, see table in Appendix Two.

Hours: 7:00 am to 10:00 pm.

Rules: Pets on leash; no alcohol.

Fees: None.

Facilities: A couple of picnic tables but no water and no camping.

Nearby Places of Interest: Old Tucson; Arizona-Sonora Desert Museum; Saguaro National Monument (West).

Comments:

This is the premier sunset watching place in Tucson and it draws crowds. Still, if you are willing to walk far enough you will surely find a private place.

In the foreground you see Old Tucson, covered elsewhere in this guide. Looking west across the Avra Valley, the mountains in the distance are all located on the Tohono O'Odham Indian Reservation which stretches west for over 80 miles. If it is clear you may be able to see the observatory buildings on Kitt Peak just off to your left in the distance. Farther south, the distinctive summit you see is Baboquivari, home of the Tohono O'Odham Indian God and Creator, I'Itoi.

Just south of Baboquivari is the Mexican border. Contemplate, if you will, that Mexicans and others from Central America commonly walk north from the border following desert routes all the way to Phoenix in search of work.

This is a great location to get shots of summer thunderstorms dumping their rain on the valley. Remember though, that there is a high risk of lightning even if the storms are five miles away.

🏛️SAGUARO NATIONAL MONUMENT(West)

Area of Town: West.
Map Reference: D 2; see also map next page.
Phone Number: 602-883-6366 (Monument Headquarters).
Directions: From the north side of town, take Ina Rd. west past I-10 until it ends, then go left on Wade Rd. which shortly turns into Picture Rocks Rd. and keep going almost seven miles to the stop sign at Sandario Rd. Take a left and go about 3.6 miles to Kinney Rd. and turn left. In about 1.8 miles you'll come to the Visitor Center.

If you are prepared for a long, slow dirt road ride you can take the "short cut" by turning left onto **Golden Gate Road** about 2 miles after you enter the Monument on Picture Rocks Rd. This eventually intersects with Sandario Rd. where you make a left and then another left on Kinney Rd. a short ways later, arriving at the Visitors Center in 2.5 miles. From the central part of town drive over Gates Pass (see direction in preceding section) to the stop sign at Kinney Rd. Take a right and go about 4.8 twisting and beautiful miles to the Visitors Center.

From the south side of town, go west on Ajo Rd. (Hwy. 86) to Kinney Rd. Turn right and drive north about 5 miles to the Visitors Center.

Best Time of Year: All Year.
Best Time of Day: Sunset, see table in Appendix Two.
Hours: 24 hours.
Rules: Pets must be leashed and are not allowed on trails.
Fees: None.
Facilities: Restrooms and drinking water. Visitors Center has ranger on duty and sells maps and books. Picnicking but no camping.
Nearby Places of Interest: Arizona-Sonora Desert Museum; Old Tucson; Gates Pass.

Comments:

This is a huge area which contains the finest giant saguaro forest in the world. For sunset viewing I suggest you drive the **Bajada Loop Drive** which starts about 1.6 miles north of the Visitors Center. This is a good graded dirt road. It is two-way for about a mile to the **Hugh Norris Trailhead** so you don't have to drive the entire six-mile loop if you don't want to. There are a number of low hills you can hike to get good views. If you prefer, the trail above the **Sus Picnic Area**, the **Valley View Trail** or the **Hugh Norris Trail** allow for excellent viewing.

Another possibility is the Golden Gate Road. (See directions above).

Facing Page: Sunset at Gates Pass

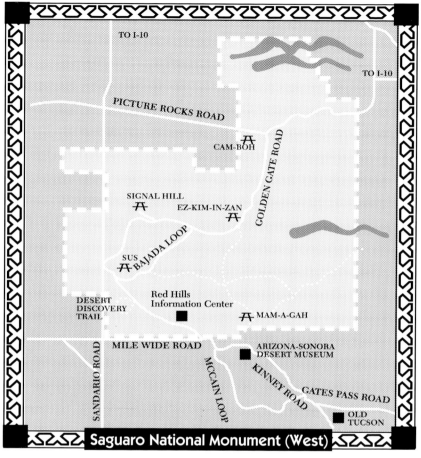

Saguaro National Monument (West)

CATALINA STATE PARK

Area of Town: Northwest.
Map Reference: B 7; see also map page 36.
Phone Number: 602-628-5798 (Park headquarters).
Directions: Located on Oracle Rd. (Hwy 80/89), about 12 miles north of downtown Tucson or about 5 miles north of Ina Rd.
Best Time of Year: All year.
Best Time of Day: Sunset, see table in Appendix Two.
Hours: 7:00 am to 10:00 pm.
Rules: Pets permitted on leash.
Fees: $3.00 per vehicle.
Facilities: Restrooms and drinking water. There are good camping and picnicking facilities, including RV spaces.
Nearby Places of Interest: Tohono Chul Park.

Comments:

There are many choices here. From most of the hills you will be able to see the sunset looking west. Many will also give a good view of the glow on the mountains. My favorite spot takes a bit of walking (about 30 min.). Park in the lot at the end of the road. Take the trailhead for Romero Trail and Sutherland Trails but just after you cross the Sutherland Wash (sometimes you'll have to wade, it's shallow and sandy) take the **Birding Loop Trail**. When you reach the loop go left and you'll soon encounter a "staircase" of railroad ties going up a hill. Shortly after this, an old dirt road intersects the loop. Go left on this track which is now an equestrian trail (not on the official park map). It changes to a trail then a sandy wash and eventually back into a trail which crosses **Alamo Canyon** just above a nice waterfall. From here there are good views west and back up Alamo Canyon to **Leviathan Dome** and **Wilderness Dome** behind it.

If you're not in the mood for walking that far, just go up the hill on the **Romero Trail** a short way and you'll get a fine view.

PONTATOC RIDGE

Area of Town: North Central.
Map Reference: C 7.
Phone Number: None.
Directions: Pontatoc Ridge is located near the north end of Alvernon Way. Unfortunately Alvernon Way does not run continuously from town to its northern terminus. To get to the section which does lead to the north end you have to start at Skyline Drive. So, go north on Swan Rd. to Skyline Dr. then left to Alvernon Way (ignoring the turn for Alvernon Circle just before) and make a right, then go to the end of the road. You also can get there by going north on Skyline where it intersects with Sunrise just east of Campbell Ave.

  Once you are at the road end you'll see a trailhead for the **Finger Rock Canyon Trail**. Just east (to the right) is another well-used trail which heads over toward the big distinctive ridge called Pontatoc Ridge. This is where you are going.

Best Time of Year: All year.
Best Time of Day: Sunset, see table in Appendix Two.
Hours: Technically parking is restricted from 10:00 pm to 6:00 am unless you get a hiking permit from Pima County Parks and Recreation Department (740-2690).
Rules: Pets on leash.
Fees: None.
Facilities: None, but there is a 24 -hour 7-11 store at Skyline & Swan.
Nearby Places of Interest: Westin La Paloma Resort, located just south on Sunrise Dr. between Swan and Campbell; definitely worth seeing, good "coffee shop." East a few miles on Sunrise Dr. and north on Kolb Rd. is **Ventana Canyon Resort**, also definitely worth seeing and also with a good "coffee shop."

Comments:

This is the most centrally located place to see the sunset. The views of the sunset are not as spectacular as from the Tucson Mountains but there are great city views and the shadows forming in the huge canyons above are awesome. After you hike in on the trail to Pontatoc Ridge a short ways you'll see a trail to the left which goes up a small pointy hill. There is a clear view of the sunset from here except from about mid-April till about mid-July when the sun sets too far north to actually see the sun sink into the western horizon. Even when you can't see the sun actually go down you will enjoy a super light show.

Facing Page: City lights at sunset © Randy Prentice

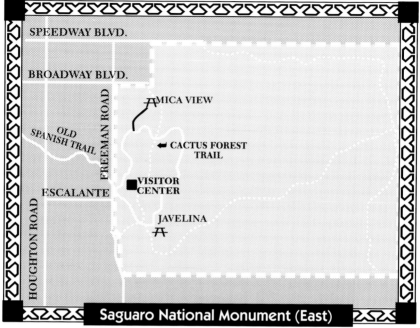

Saguaro National Monument (East)

SAGUARO NATIONAL MONUMENT(East)

Area of Town: East.

Map Reference: E 8.

Phone Number: 602-296-8576, Saguaro National Monument (East).

Directions: Take Broadway or Speedway east to Houghton Road and go right to **Old Spanish Trail** and follow it to the Visitors Center of the Saguaro National Monument (East).

Best Time of Year: All year.

Best Time of Day: Sunset, see table in Appendix Two.

Hours: The mountains are open for business 24 hours, but the Cactus Forest Drive in Saguaro National Monument (East) is only open from 7:00 am to 7:00 pm. If you are on the loop drive by 7:00 pm you may stay until dark. The Visitors Center is open from 8:00 am to 5:00 pm.

Rules: No pets on the trails in Saguaro National Monument.

Fees: One vehicle is $4.00; bikes and buses pay $2.00 per person; an annual pass for the Monument only is $10.00; Golden Access pass, good at all National Parks and Monuments is $25.00; Golden Age Pass Holders, free.

Facilities: Restrooms; picnic areas but no camping.

Nearby Places of Interest: Follow Old Spanish Trail south a few miles to Colossal Cave which has a regular tour.

Comments:

The Monument is a little higher than the Tucson Valley and offers an unobstructed view of the entire valley and the Tucson Mountains. No matter what the time of year, there is a direct view of the sun going down from several spots on the loop drive. Especially popular are **Javelina Rocks**, a group of large granite outcroppings near the 6-mile point on the loop drive.

If it is quiet, you may be able to use the position on the rocks to spot coyotes start their evening hunt.

WINDY POINT

Area of Town: Catalina Mountains, Northeast of Town.
Map Reference: B 12; see also map page 39.
Phone Number: 602-749-8700 (Santa Catalina Ranger District).
Directions: Take Tanque Verde Rd. east to the Catalina Highway, go left and follow the road up the mountain to milepost 14 where the road makes a sharp turn to the right and park in the lot on the right. If the lot is full, keep going a couple of hundred yards and park at Geology Vista and hike the trail back to Windy Point.
Best Time of Year: All year, but depending on the weather. If it is cold and rainy in town, it will be unpleasant at Windy Point.
Best Time of Day: Late afternoon; Sunset, see table in Appendix Two.
Hours: 24 Hours.
Rules: Pets on leash.
Fees: None.
Facilities: None at Windy Point but there is picnicking at Bear Canyon and camping at Molino Basin and General Hitchcock before Windy Point, and at Rose Canyon Lake farther up the highway.
Nearby Places of Interest: On the way up the mountain you will pass through **Molino Canyon** and **Bear Canyon** which offer great canyon scenery. A stop to explore the creeks running through these canyons is worthwhile. **Rose Canyon Lake** is a small manmade lake located just off the highway at a popular campground. It is surprisingly photogenic.

Comments:

Windy Point is the place where the Catalina Highway traverses west up a ridge of granite cliffs and spires and then makes a 180 degree turn back. At the point of the turn there is a parking lot and easy access to a view point complete with guard rails.

Get here early to watch the **rock climbers**. The late afternoon light on the cliffs and spires with the sometimes outrageously clad climbers can make

for great photos. There is a short "practice cliff" just below the lookout where newcomers are taught to rappel and climb.

Hitchcock Pinnacle just above the parking lot presents a splendid photo opportunity, especially if there are climbers on it, and there often are. Hike up the hill until you are just above it and you will get a great shot with the valley in the background.

Also, there is a short hiking route which leads farther out the point with good views and less crowding. It is not a constructed trail but it is easy walking. It starts across the road at far end of the parking lot, just right of the guard rail, and traverses out to the end of the ridge. Generally, bear right and avoid climbing down any cliffs--there are some long drops here.

You will often hear rock climbers before you see them. The climbing routes are hard to find because of the complex series of rock fins and spires, but you can usually follow the voices. Be very careful not to kick or throw rocks off the tops of cliffs as even a small rock will pierce a climber's unhelmeted skull and they hate it when that happens.

If you are a rock climber there is world-class climbing here. Pick up *Squeezing the Lemmon, A Rock Climber's Guide to the Mt. Lemmon Highway* at the Summit Hut on Speedway or at the several Bob's Bargain Barn locations. There are many other fine climbing locations throughout southern Arizona which are described in *Backcountry Rockclimbing in Southern Arizona* also available at the Summit Hut and Bob's.

Sunset at Windy Point is different than it is from in the Valley. The angle to the horizon is totally different and so is the effect on light. The light tends to be more finely spun with an ethereal effect rather than the bright Kodachrome colors of a true desert sunset. Still, the stacking of the ridges in the foreground and the mountain ranges in the distance can make memorable images.

Photo tips: Slow shutter speeds and **slow film** (no faster than ISO 100) are the key to the best sunset photos, especially in weak winter light. With fast film the subtle variance in light is difficult to capture and the color saturation will be thin. You will need your **tripod** of course, as the light is weaker the prettier it gets. If you don't have one, set the camera on a rock and use the self timer, or at least brace your hands on a rock.

This may be a good place to experiment with a **graduated split neutral density filter**. This is a device that fits over the front of the lens like other filters but is split in two halves, a light and a dark, typically about two f-stops different with a graduated zone between them. The idea is to have the dark part cover the sky and the light part cover the foreground so the details in the foreground will come out instead of being reproduced as a dark outline, which would be the result without the filter. Like other experiments suggested here, be sure to back up your shots with methods you are sure of so you don't go home without at least a record shot.

Facing Page:Sunset from Windy Point, © *Peter Noebels*

To someone on vacation or even your average citizen on their weekend day off, the idea of rising in the predawn hour to rush off somewhere to commune with nature and/or take photographs may seem a little radical. But it is the best time of day in the desert for much of the year. **Sunrise times** are in Appendix Two.

I must confess that when it is cold or inclement in the winter, I rarely see the dawn except from the window of the breakfast nook in our foothills home. But still, I've gotten some unbelievable photos of the eastern sky lit up with gorgeous hues even in the dead of winter (or what passes for the dead of winter in Tucson).

In the warm weather though, the first hour or so of the day is charmed. First, there may be a light show in the eastern sky. Then, the sunlight spreads over the desert like magic, long shadows creeping before it. The spines of the cholla cactus radiate the backlight as if they were spun of glass. The birds sing their welcome to the day, and it is cool enough to wander the desert in comfort. The world seems at peace.

For the photographer, the light of early morning pays special rewards. The same desert that yields harsh, flat photos at mid-day, rewards the early riser with rich, saturated colors and soft shadows that can produce compelling images on film.

When it is really hot in Tucson from mid-June to mid-September, the early hour is a further blessing for taking photographs or wandering the desert. With afternoon temperatures of well over 100 degrees it is an effort to breathe, much less hike around to see the sights or take photos.

The best view of sunrise is from **Wasson Peak** in the Tucson mountains but that involves a predawn hike of 5 miles with a 1900-foot elevation gain. Surprisingly enough, this is somewhat of a Tucson classic and you may well have company at dawn on Wasson Peak.

At the opposite extreme you can get a great roadside view from **Picture Rocks Rd**. just inside the **Saguaro National Monument(West)**. There are also some good places to scramble up the hills nearby to get better views.

Sabino Canyon is also convenient, and has great cactus stands and flowers to explore while watching the day begin. You probably will not get an actual view of the sunrise in the warmer months because the sun comes up behind the Santa Catalina Mountains at that time of year. But, in the winter there is a fine view, and even in the summer the early morning light is fantastic in the canyon. The bird life at Sabino Canyon is especially active and there are deer who seem to have no fear.

Finally, there are numerous locations in the Catalina Foothills, including several fine hotels, where the early light can be enjoyed without much inconvenience. In fact, the most unobstructed sunrise view I've found is from the roof of our foothills home, but my wife Lynn says not to invite everyone over.

Photo Tips: As with sunset, the soft light of dawn results in slow shutter speeds which require a tripod, bracing the camera, or use of the self timer. Again, if you don't overdo it, **fill flash** may enhance your efforts if you are trying to capture something like a cactus in the foreground with the dawn behind. It will prevent the cactus from being a black outline. Personally, I find fill flash to be tricky so I always make sure I've taken the best photo I can with natural light before I try to enhance the image by filling in the shadows with flash. Fill flash is most worthwhile to fill in some detail while still getting the wonderful backlighting effects produced as the early sun rises through cactus and flowers. If you have a separate flash unit, the best results for fill flash will be produced if you get an off-camera cord so you can hold the flash at a distance from the camera and at an angle to the subject.

Get there early. The dawn gives its best sky colors before the sun appears above the horizon, so get to your viewpoint at least 30 minutes before official sunrise. Check the sunrise table in Appendix Two. Don't forget to use your flashlight to check for crawly things if its dark--this is their time of day. Also, take something warm to wear in the cool predawn.

Sunrise over the Rincon Mountains

PICTURE ROCKS ROAD

Area of Town: Northwest.
Map Reference: D 3; see map page 12.
Phone Number: 602-883-6366, Saguaro National Monument (West)
Directions: Take Ina Road west from I-10 to Wade Rd., then turn left and follow it to Picture Rocks Rd. Just after the sign for the National Monument park in one of the pulloffs. A note of caution—this seemingly quiet desert road is used by the folks in the Avra Valley to commute to work in Tucson and they are frequently in a big hurry— don't get in their way!
Best Time of Year: All year.
Best Time of Day: Sunrise, see table in Appendix Two.
Hours: 24 Hours.
Rules: No pets on trais.
Fees: None.
Facilities: None.
Nearby Places of Interest: You'll probably want coffee at the 24-hour Circle K on Ina just east of I-10; on the trip back, the Donut Wheel next door should be open.

Comments:

There are no official facilities here, no trails or lookouts. You can park in the pullout just past the National Monument sign and then hike up the hill on the south side of the road. There are many good places to view the sunrise, but if you want to get the best views of the early sun on Wasson Peak and the rest of the Tucson Mountains, continue up to the little peak. It is a **short but stiff hike**.

The other alternative is to continue up the road another couple of hundred yards to the big pullout at the pass. You can get a picture from next to the car but I'd suggest making the effort to scramble up the steep loose slope to the top of the little peak just north of the pass. Here you will get excellent views of the sunrise and Wasson Peak as well as good views to the north and west.

Facing Page: Backlite saguaro, Saguaro National Monument (West),
©Randy Prentice

WASSON PEAK

Area of Town: West.

Map Reference: D 3; see also map page 12.

Phone Number: 602-883-6366, Saguaro National Monument (West).

Directions: The most direct way to get to the trailheads is from the north side of town. Take Ina Rd. west past I-10 to its terminus at Wade Rd. Go left on Wade and it soon turns into Picture Rocks Rd. which you follow into the Monument. If you are going to use the **Sendero Esperanza Trailhead** (see comment) turn left on Golden Gate Road about 2 miles west of the monument boundary. The trailhead is about 3 miles from Picture Rocks Rd. and it is well signed.

Best Time of Year: All year.

Best Time of Day: Sunrise, see table in Appendix Two.

Hours: 24 hours.

Rules: No pets on trails.

Fees: None.

Facilities: Restrooms at the trailheads.

Nearby Places of Interest: You'll probably want coffee at the 24-hour Circle K on Ina just east of I-10.

Comments:

I debated long and hard about putting this location in this guide because very few of the other suggestions require the amount of commitment this one does. But if you are willing to **start a few hours before dawn** the reward is one of the best sunrise locations I've ever seen. The sun shadows creeping up the canyons on the east side of the Tucson Mountains make the hike worthwhile even if there isn't a colorful sky show in the East. Also the hike back down will be in great light and the desert vegetation is outstanding.

The **Sendero Esperanza Trail** is the shortest and even allowing for the dark (there is usually a pretty good glow from Tucson so it's not really all that dark) you should be able to make the top in two hours from the trailhead. The Hugh Norris Trail is a little longer, but a nice gentle grade all the same. Allow another 20 or 30 minutes to hike it.

If you can, it's worthwhile to do the hike in the moonlight. Regardless, be sure to take a reliable flashlight, extra batteries and something warm to wear even if you do it in the warm weather because the peak is 4,687 feet and will be cool in the predawn.

▦⛭▦⛭▦⛭▦⛭SABINO CANYON

Area of Town: Northeast.

Map Reference: C 9; see also Hiking Map page 32.

Phone Number: 602-749-8700 (Santa Catalina Ranger District) 749-2861 (Shuttle Bus Information).

Directions: Take Sunrise Rd. east to Sabino Canyon Rd., turn left and the entrance is the next right. Or take Tanque Verde Rd. east, then turn left on Sabino Canyon Rd. and follow it to the canyon.

Best Time of Year: All year.

Best Time of Day: Sunrise, see table in Appendix Two.

Hours: 24 Hours.

Tram runs from 9:00 am to 4:30 pm on the hour M-F, on the half hour in Sabino Canyon weekends and holidays; 9:00 am to 4:00 pm on the hour to Lower Sabino and Lower Bear Canyon.

Rules: No pets; no glass containers.

Fees: None; Tram is $5.00 for adults, $2.00 for children to Sabino Canyon; $3.00 & $1.25 for Lower Sabino and Lower Bear Canyons.

Facilities: Drinking water, restrooms, tram, picnic areas, Visitors Center.

Nearby Places of Interest: Ventana Canyon Resort is located west on Sunrise Rd. and north on Kolb. It is worth seeing and is a place to treat yourself to a fancy, expensive breakfast.

Comments:

To get sunrise views you will have to leave the paved road and hike a short ways. There are several ridges that offer good views of the sunrise when it is setting far enough south. In the warmer weather though it sets behind the Santa Catalinas and there won't be a view of the actual sunrise here.

One of the things that makes this a special place to be at dawn is the shadow and light show in the canyon. Also, when there is a direct sunrise here there are great stands of saguaros on the ridges to dress up your photos. Another special treat is the backlighting of the saguaros, chollas and other cactus as the sun's rays bend around the cactus spines and create an unearthly aura.

CATALINA FOOTHILLS

Area of Town: North.

Map Reference: C 7-8.

Directions: Go north on Campbell, Swan or Craycroft until they reach the mountains. See more specific directions in Comments below.

Best Time of Year: All year.

Best Time of Day: Sunrise, see table in Appendix Two.

Hours: There are signs saying parking is restricted between 6:00 pm and 6:00 am but they are there to discourage late night revelers and are not strictly enforced.

Rules: Pets on leash.

Fees: None.

Facilities: None.

Nearby Places of Interest: Westin La Paloma Resort on Sunrise between Campbell and Swan has beautiful grounds and a good "coffee shop." Likewise for the Ventana Canyon Resort located east on Sunrise and north on Kolb Rd.

Comments:

North Campbell Ave. Follow Campbell Ave. north to its end at the Cobblestone subdivision. There is a miserable National Forest access here but that's not what you came for. Instead just park in the public spots and make the most of the city view. Like the other Catalina Foothills locations here there will not be a direct sunrise view in the warmer weather, but the light coming over the city is pretty and you didn't have to walk to see it.

North Alvernon Way. From Campbell Ave. go east on Sunrise and then go north (left) on the Skyline Rd. turnoff. Follow that to Alvernon Way and go north (left) to the end. Basically the same view as North Campbell from the car but here you have the option the hike up the **Finger Rock Canyon Trail** or the **Pontatoc Ridge Trail** a ways to get much better views.

North Swan Rd. There is no public parking, but there are places to pull over with comfort. Also, there is a good French Bakery in the shopping center at the southeast corner of Sunrise and Swan. Really, about the only thing you can say about the views here are that they are easy to get to. I'd suggest you make the commitment to do a little walking and try one of the other locations unless you are really limited for time.

T he steep, dramatic canyons of the Santa Catalina Mountains command affection, awe, and even fear. Viewed from a distance, they lend modeling to the mountains, giving them an ever changing aspect in the desert sun. To the family basking in the warmth alongside the tree-lined creek in Sabino Canyon the atmosphere is friendly and quiet. To the hiker clinging to a trail along a canyon wall a feeling of awe can be on the borderline with fear, imposed by the cliffs looming above and the void below.

None of the locations covered in this hapter encompass the last category of danger. They were selected to cover a variety of canyon experiences and photographic opportunities. This coverage only scratches the surface of what is available in Southern Arizona. I urge you to seek out alternatives using the resources listed in Appendix Nine. For example, **Sabino Canyon** is known by every Tucsonan but few have ever heard of, much less visited, **Breakfast Canyon** just to the west. True, it doesn't have the big creek but it does have seasonal water and its own unique beauty. Most importantly, it is uncrowded, in sharp contrast to Sabino on most days.

The canyons listed in this section are all big ones in the Santa Catalina Mountains. There are plenty more of every size and character in the Rincon, Santa Rita, Tucson and Tortolita mountains. The **Summit Hut**, 5045 E. Speedway, is a good place to research their excellent collection of guides and maps to these areas. The employees are knowledgeable and will take time to help with your questions. Plus, they have the best collection of outdoor gear in town.

Busy or not, **Sabino Canyon** must head the list of any canyon experience in the Tucson area. It has dramatic cliffs, huge green trees, a cool creek and a road with a tram right up the middle. Hiking the road is also nice, you can enjoy the sights and sounds of early morning or late evening without having to watch your footing every second. You will especially like it if you treat yourself to a moonlight walk up the canyon. Also, it's a non-threatening place to take anyone who otherwise might be nervous about treading a rocky desert trail.

Sabino Canyon does offer more natural ways to explore it. I'd urge anyone to try the **Phone Line Trail** which contours along the east side of the canyon. After a moderate uphill hike the trail levels out and allows wonderful views of the canyon and a more intimate experience with the flora and fauna of the desert.

Pima Canyon is more open than Sabino and seems more livable. Native Americans apparently agreed, and in the bedrock near the pool about three miles up the trail you can see shallow dishes in the rock where they ground mesquite beans for food. Shady groves of huge old cotton-wood trees along the creek make good rest spots.

The wonderful sculpted granite pools of **Romero Canyon** in Catalina State Park draw many regular visitors. It is a pleasant hike to the pools, but not as easy as getting around in Sabino Canyon.

Photo Tips: Pay attention to low shutter speeds if the canyon is in deep shade. Remember the rule that the shutter speed should not be lower than the focal length of your lens. For example, if your lens is 50mm you should not try to hand hold the camera if the shutter speed is less than 1/60; with a 100mm lens shoot with at least 1/125, if hand held. To take sharp pictures in low light be prepared with a tripod, brace the camera or set the camera on a rock and use the self timer. If it is shady, you might consider a "**warming filter**" like a #81B to reduce the blue cast of the shade and give the photo a more pleasant feel.

SABINO CANYON

PIMA CANYON

Area of Town: Northeast.

Map Reference: C 7: see map next page.

Phone Number: 602-749-8700 (Santa Catalina Ranger District).

Directions: Go north on N. First Ave. to Ina Rd. then continue north on Christie Dr. and make a right where it ends at Magee Rd. Take a right and continue east to the parking at the trailhead. Or, drive east on Magee Rd. from N. Oracle Rd. Note, once the new hotel is built at the mouth of Pima Canyon, the parking will be different but there should be signs to the new trail head which is being planned as part of the development.

Best Time of Year: Fall, Winter, Spring. From mid-June to early October it will be too hot except in the early morning.

Best Time of Day: The light is always the best in the first few hours in the morning and the last few in the afternoon. In winter the weaker light can be pleasant at mid-day and you won't freeze.

Hours: 24 hours, but the parking is restricted from 10:00 pm to 6:00 am.

Rules: Pets on leash.

Fees: None.

Facilities: None.

Nearby Places of Interest: Catalina State Park just north on Oracle Road has good picnic facilities and easier access to water. Tohono Chul Park is even closer and has an excellent restaurant as well as peaceful desert paths to stroll.

Comments:

I t is a dry walk into the canyon for a half mile or so, but the reward is a creek which flows a fair amount of the time through restful groves of giant cottonwoods. The canyon is open and quite long. The first few miles are level, anyone can do this hike.

Walking in a mile or so will put you squarely in the canyon with its spectacular views. The canyon is in the **Pusch Ridge Wilderness Area**. To your left as you walk in is **Table Mountain**, home to many of the Catalina's **desert bighorn sheep**. While they are shy, they are occasionally seen. The ewes and kids usually stay together and the rams roam in a separate small herd. The sight of several bighorn rams strutting around like body builders on the rocky cliff tops is not soon forgotten. You are unlikely to get close enough for a good photograph, but bring your binoculars and a long lens just in case.

About three miles in you will come on a little stone dam in the creek. To the right a hundred feet or so are some smooth dished spots in the bedrock called **metates** where the Indians ground their food from mesquite beans.

If you are an avid hiker you can follow the trail to the top of **Mt. Kimball** (7255'). This is a strenuous hike taking three or four hours up and two to three down. The 4,500-foot gain in elevation is comparable to hiking out of the Grand Canyon. Take plenty of water and energy food, a map, something warm to wear and a flashlight. Your reward will be a phenomenal view into the rugged west side of the Catalinas.

An alternate to the hike up to Mt. Kimball is **Table Mountain** (6250'). Just past the stone dam you will encounter a drainage on your left leading up to the top of Table Mountain. This is a strenuous hike and there is no trail. But if you have the time and energy the cliff at the north side of Table Mountain may be the most exposed, dramatic spot in all of the Catalinas (except for the top of Finger Rock). The views of the giant granite domes to the north include Leviathan and Wilderness Domes set in a forest of peaks and spires. Have warm clothes, at least two quarts of water, a flashlight and high energy food. Tell someone where you are going and when you expect to be back.

Hike up the gully and turn right uphill through shindagger fields and then oak, piñon and juniper forest for another hour or two to the top. The distance to the top from the trailhead is 4.5 miles but because much of it is not on trail the going is pretty difficult. Allow 8 hours round trip from the car if you are in reasonable shape. There is a trail register near the middle of the cliff.

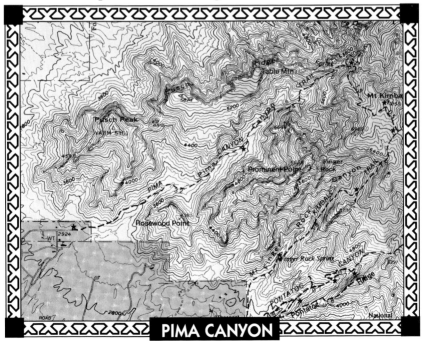

PIMA CANYON

Canyons

ROMERO CANYON

Area of Town: Northwest.

Map Reference: B 7; see also map next page.

Phone Number: 602-628-5798 (Park Headquarters).

Directions: Located in Catalina State Park on Oracle Rd. (Hwy 80/89), about 12 miles north of downtown Tucson or about 5 miles north of Ina Rd.

Best Time of Year: March through May and August through October will be the best time to find water running and get good wildflower viewing. August and September are hot, but there are often cooling respites after thunderstorms.

Best Time of Day: Early and late for good light, but if it's cold you may want to wait until the sun has warmed up the canyon bottom.

Hours: 7:00 am to 10:00 pm.

Rules: Pets on leash.

Fees: $3.00 per vehicle.

Facilities: Restrooms and drinking water. There are good camping and picnicking facilities, including RV spaces.

Nearby Places of Interest: Go north on Highway 89 and then right at Oracle Junction on Highway 77 and you will encounter Biosphere 2. Closer to town is the Sheraton El Conquistador Resort which has fine views and good food.

Comments:

The big attractions in Romero Canyon are the little falls and clear pools in marble-like granite. There is a sensual feel to the sun-warmed granite which has been polished by eons of seasonal water flow. In the spring there will be great wildflowers.

It can be hot here, so if it seems too warm when you get out of the car, give it up; it won't be any cooler trudging up the trail. Most folks just hike until they find a pool that appeals and call it a hike. It is possible to hike to the top of **Mt. Lemmon** (9,157') but it would take most of the day for a very strong hiker and leave no time for a return in the light.

To beat the crowds you might take a side trip up **Montrose Canyon** which you will encounter coming in from the right about 2.8 miles up the Romero Trail. There is no trail but you can't get lost because the canyon is so steep you couldn't wander out if you wanted to.

Photo Tips: The flowers and critters which are attracted to the little pools offer many possibilities for close-up photography. If you have a **macro** lens or a zoom with a macro setting you have it made. If not, don't despair. You may be able to use an inexpensive set of close-up lenses which screw on your lens like regular filters and work very well.

If it is breezy (it always is when the flowers are the most beautiful) try your **flash**; if done right it may freeze the action. It will also be helpful when shooting in the shade. If you camera will "sync" at 1/125th or 1/250th use those settings with the flash. If in doubt, do a little experimenting but take some shots without the flash as well because it is a tricky process to figure out your equipment. When mastered, the process of using flash for macro photography will produce great results even in difficult lighting conditions and breezy weather.

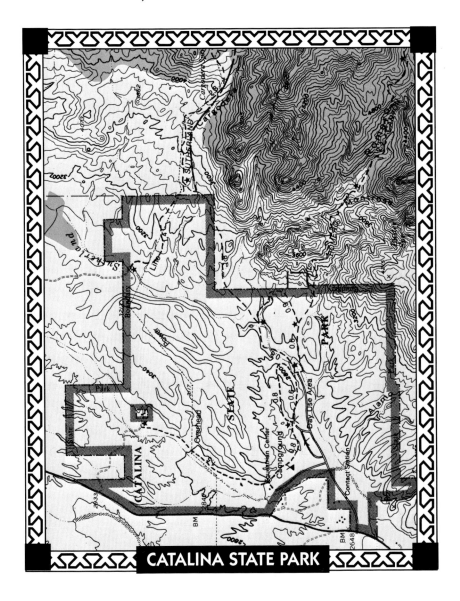

CATALINA STATE PARK

T
ucson is a city of mountains, ringed in on all sides by ragged peaks, some close, some in the near distance. In the north, the Front Range of the Santa Catalina Mountains looms over the Catalina Foothills neighborhoods. The Rincon Mountains massively describe the east edge of town. To the south the sentinel of Mount Wrightson "Old Baldy" identifies the Santa Rita Mountains. The stark Tucson Mountains spill almost into the downtown business district.

Since you cannot avoid seeing the mountains it may seem a little silly to have a section in a guidebook to Tucson talking about them. But, it is easy to find yourself constantly looking at the mountains through a filter of residential streets, or highway traffic, and miss their true majesty. By guiding you to a few favorite mountain places I hope you will be encouraged to get out and find your own special spots.

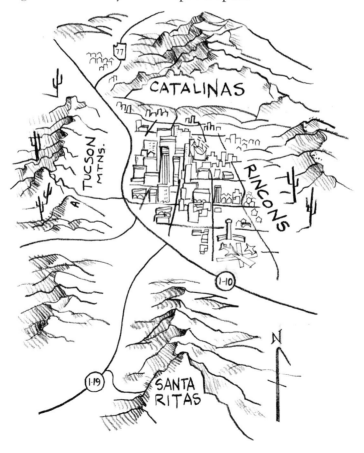

Santa Catalina Mountains

The **Santa Catalina Mountains** get the most coverage because they are the closest and offer the most variety and easiest access. They encompass over 200 square miles, including an incredible variety of vegetation ranging from saguaros in the foothills to towering Douglas fir on the cool north slopes of 9,157-foot Mount Lemmon.

The **Front Range** includes that section of the Catalinas seen to the north of most of Tucson. It can best be visualized as a great ridge running east and west, anchored on the west by **Pusch Ridge** near Oro Valley and extending east to **Sabino Canyon**. Behind, lays another and bigger "ridge" which the Catalina Highway follows as it winds its way to the top of the range at Mount Lemmon.

Mount Kimball at 7,255 feet, is the focal point for the dramatic formations that catch the morning and evening light above Finger Rock Canyon near the north end of Alvernon Way. **Prominent Point, Finger Rock, Finger Rock Guard** and the **Thumb** are some of these formations. **Rosewood Point** just down and to the left is named for the rosy light it catches in the sunset.

The **Mount Lemmon Highway** is also called the **Catalina Highway** or the **General Hitchcock Highway**. It is one of the most dramatic roads anywhere as it winds upward, clinging to narrow canyons and traversing knife-edge ridges of fantastic granite spires. Finally, it cruises through dense Ponderosa pine forests and ends at a ski area which gets a hundred inches or more of snow over a winter season. Along the way scenic wonders make it difficult to keep your eyes on the road, with the result that this is the most dangerous stretch of road in Pima County.

The **Summit Crags** are a group of huge granite outcroppings near the top of Mount Lemmon. They offer a way to get out of the pine forest to enjoy the view of the mountains and the valley below. For many years the Forest Service has made use of their position as a location for the fire lookout cabin on the top of **Lemmon Rock**. It is a pleasant place to visit and is easier to get to than the other summit crags, **Rappel Rock, The Ravens** or **The Fortress**. Also, during the spring, Lemmon Lookout may be the only Summit Crag open to visitors as the others may be closed to hikers and climbers to protect the nesting **peregrine falcons.**

Rincon Mountains

The massive Rincon Mountains are very different than the Santa Catalinas. They are not as rugged and access is much more restricted. There is no road running to the top. Getting deep into its canyons requires a very long hike. Nonetheless they provide some wonderful moody views, especially in the winter when the big Pacific storms pass through Southern Arizona.

Mountains

Santa Rita Mountains

This range is definitely worth the drive to explore. There is a road which goes up Madera Canyon to the 5,400 foot level, and there are two trails (one easy and one steep) to the top of 9,453 foot Mount Wrightson. The birding in Madera Canyon is world-class with species that are not seen elsewhere in the United States.

Tucson Mountains

These mountains probably look like the real "Old West" to you. That may be because you grew up seeing the Tucson Mountains as a backdrop in western movies that were filmed at **Old Tucson**, the movie location on the west side of the range. From Rio Lobo with John Wayne to Young Guns with today's hot young stars, many miles of film have been shot featuring the saguaros and ragged peaks of the Tucson Mountains, with good and bad guys fighting it out in the corrals, streets, and buildings of bygone days.

There are excellent walking trails in the Tucson Mountains and the jagged rock formations make fitting backdrops to the wild cactus displays. This is the warmest place to see the mountains in the winter but also the hottest in summer.

"A" Mountain is the conical little mountain that overlooks downtown Tucson. There is a road leading to the top and the views of the valley are excellent. The big "A" is painted white each year by freshpersons from the University of Arizona. It is also occasionally surreptitiously painted ASU Sundevil colors of maroon and gold before the big intrastate football game. St. Patty has also been known to cause the "A" to appear green in March.

MOUNT LEMMON HIGHWAY
(AKA Catalina Highway or General Hitchcock Highway)

Area of Town: Northeast.

Map Reference: C, B, 11-12; see also map next page.

Phone Number: 602-749-8700 (Santa Catalina Ranger District).

Directions: Take Grant or Speedway east to Tanque Verde. Continue on Tanque Verde to the Catalina Highway sign, then go left and follow the road for 30 miles as it winds up the mountain. Fill up with gas before you go, there is no gas at the top of Mount Lemmon.

Best Time of Year: All year, but it depends where you are on the mountain. The top will always be a lot cooler, see Appendix Three. The lower canyons will be too hot in the summer except for the early morning. Sometimes in winter, chains or four wheel drive will be required above the point where the road is covered with snow or ice.

Best Time of Day: It depends on the time of year and where you are on the mountain. Above Molino Basin it will stay cool until midday in the winter.

Hours: 24 hours.

Rules: Pets on leash; take all your trash back down with you; do not drink and drive anywhere but especially not on the Mount Lemmon Highway.

Fees: None, camping in Forest Service campgrounds is $7.00 per night.

Facilities: Several good picnic areas along the road have rest rooms and drinking water. Camping is available at Rose Canyon Lake, General Hitchcock and Molino Basin. There are a couple of small lodge/bed & breakfast type places to stay at Summerhaven, the village at the top. Also, there are several really good places to eat at the top. My favorite is the chili at the Iron Door Restaurant located at the ski valley.

Nearby Places of Interest: With all that there is to do on Mount Lemmon you won't have time for anything else.

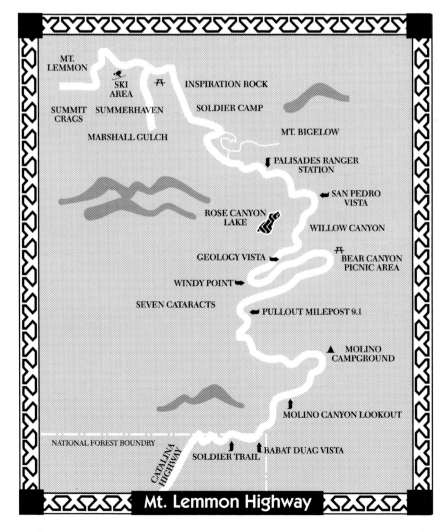

Comments:

Over its 25-mile length the Catalina Highway climbs almost 6,500 feet from 2,800 feet in the valley to 9,157 feet on the top of Mt. Lemmon. As it climbs it passes through life zones of vegetation from the lower Sonoran to Canadian. The road starts up the mountain flanked by stands of giant saguaro marching up the canyon walls. Cholla, prickly pear and ocotillo combine to make clear this is a desert. As the road climbs a few miles to **Molino Basin** (4,300') the cooler elevation is evidenced by a change of vegetation to oak, juniper and piñon woodlands, still interspersed with desert species like agave and giant century plants.

Where the road turns into the shady confines of **Upper Bear Canyon** (6,000') at milepost 10, the forest closes in and thick stands of Ponderosa pine add a wonderful spice to the air. By the time the road stops near the top of **Mt. Lemmon** at over 9,000' there are enormous Douglas fir sharing the north slopes of the forest with the Ponderosa pine and groves of quaking Aspen trees.

Started in the 1930's and finished in 1950, the Mount Lemmon Highway was built mostly by prison labor from a Federal Prison Camp. The camp was established on the mountain for the express purpose of supplying labor for the road. It was a minimum security facility and in the early days included a fair number of bootleggers. Over the 18 years it took to complete the road, more than 8,000 prisoners worked on it.

Food & Lodging

The village of Summerhaven near the top of the mountain is the center for the several hundred people who call Mt. Lemmon home. The village has two excellent restaurants, Kimball Springs and the Mt. Lemmon Café. Summerhaven Suites and Sweets (602-576-1542) offers a few rooms to rent and tasty bakery goods. Cabins can be rented by prior arrangement with Mt. Lemmon Realty (602-576-1333).

The Mt. Lemmon Ski Area offers good snow much of the winter although the slopes tend to be steep. The ski lift operates all year and is a boon to hikers who can use it to get to the top of the ridge and then hike

down the Aspen Draw and Sabino Dawn Trails. Also at the ski area is the Iron Door Restaurant with very good food and some of the best chili you will ever have. The patio has unique entertainment as dozens of hummingbirds swarm to the feeders within a few feet of the diners. Their dive bombing antics have to be seen to be believed.

Driving

As you start up the highway there is a great place to stop and take a record photograph next to the Coronado National Forest sign with **Soldier Canyon** and slopes of saguaros in the background. Also in the spring there are colorful wildflower displays.

During the 90's the highway is scheduled to be rebuilt. A section of several miles is being done every other year. Occasionally during construction there are delays or the road may even be closed for several hours in the middle of the day. Call the Forest Service for current information.(602-749-8700).

The following are suggested stops only; there are many others places that are worth seeing--just make sure you find a safe pullout before you start sightseeing.

Milepost 2.5—**Babat Duag Vista** (3,500') gives a good view of the valley.

Milepost 4.5—**Molino Canyon Lookout** (4,000')provides a good view of Molino Canyon and also access to the creek with some nice waterfalls when there is water in the creek.

Milepost 5.4—**Molino Basin Campground** (4,300') It will be too hot to do anything here in the summer except early in the day. This is a good picnic spot and there are restrooms. Across the road from the entrance is a trail which can be hiked or mountain-biked for several miles south over a ridge into the Redington Pass area. If you go that far it is very strenuous, but a nice walk can be had by staying in the canyon bottom.

Milepost 9.1—There is a **big pullout** (5,280') on the left as the road heads right into Upper Bear Canyon. From the pullout there are **good views of the valley**. In the middle distance is a distinctive little summit called **Thimble Peak** (5,323') located on a ridge between Lower Bear Canyon and Sabino Canyon. Especially in the late afternoon light, there is a wonderful layering effect as the ridges in the foreground and the distant mountain ranges stack up, each catching a different amount of the fading light. **Seven Cataracts** fall into Bear Canyon directly across from the pullout.

Milepost 11.3—**The Bear Canyon Picnic Area** (6,000') is in a forest of pine trees. It usually surprises visitors to suddenly find themselves in a shady pine forest after the canyons and open slopes below.

Milepost 14—**Windy Point Vista** (6400') offers great views of the valley and the cliffs and vertical granite spires. There are usually rock climbers creeping up the vertical walls. Just below the lookout with the railing is the practice cliff where thousands have learned to climb and rappel. **Hitchcock Pinnacle**, just above the parking lot often has climbers on it and offers a good photo opportunity without having to hike too far.

Milepost 14.4—**Geology Vista** (6,400') has an interpretative display and good views of the **Rincon Mountains**. If you walk up the road a ways, there are good views of the fantastic rock formations lining the road. Watch out for traffic, there is no shoulder.

Milepost 14.8—**Goosehead Rock**(6,400). This distinctive feature occasionally will have climbers on it, there is a route which comes up and over the beak.

Milepost 17.4—**San Pedro Vista**(7,300')looks out on the **San Pedro River Valley**. The mountains across the way are the **Galiuro Mountains** which are protected as the Galiuro Wilderness. This is one of the most untraveled ranges in Southern Arizona with one of the densest bear populations in the United States. Off to the left is the copper smelter at **San Manuel** which is a better neighbor since they curtailed much of the smoke from the stacks.

Milepost 20.8—**Mt. Bigelow Road**. This dirt road leads to the top of Mt. Bigelow (8,550'). In the winter this can be a good place to sled, tube or cross country ski. Also the **White Tail Picnic Area** just across the highway is good for a short cross country ski.

Milepost 22—**Mt. Lemmon Control Road**. This mileage is approximate, as the highway is under construction at this writing. The Control Road (Forest Road 38) is a pretty good dirt road which winds over 20 miles down the back side of the mountain to the town of Oracle. This is a long slow drive. If there is snow or if it is wet, four-wheel drive is recommended.

Milepost 23—**Road junction**, go left to Summerhaven and Marshall Gulch and right to the ski valley.

Milepost 23.2-**Summerhaven**(7,600'). The facilities in the village are discussed above.

Milepost 25—**Marshall Gulch** (7,450') is reached by going left at the road junction and continuing through Summerhaven to the end of the road. This is an area of deep forest and small canyons with creeks. Sabino Creek starts here. **The Aspen Loop Trail,** which starts from the road's end loop, is a nice hike that takes a couple of hours to do, more if you stop at the nice view points along the way. In the fall, this is golden with changing aspen trees. **The Sunset Trail** heads down Sabino Creek for a way before contouring back to the Mt. Lemmon Highway. The trailhead is at the left side of the parking lot. It soon crosses the creek and continues down the left side. Good views into the canyon start within a few hundred yards. Many people are lost by continuing down a false trail along the creek which peters out.

Milepost 25—**Mount Lemmon Ski Valley** (8,400')lies at the end of the regular highway. There is a ski lift that operates winter and summer up the ski slopes which are covered with a carpet of grass in the summer.

Mt. Lemmon Hiking

Hiking

While the grand views of the mountains can be taken in from the car, the best way to experience the Catalinas is to hike. The hikes suggested here are several of the favorites; there are many more. The most complete trail guide to the Catalinas is Pete Cowgill's & Eber Glendening's, *Trail Guide to the Santa Catalina Mountains.* **The Southern Arizona Hiking Club** produces an excellent topographic trail map of the Catalinas which is available in local outdoor stores like the Summit Hut on Speedway. If you are interested in hiking, the club is a great way to start. They produce a monthly newsletter listing all the planned outings which vary from very easy nature walks to 30-mile death marches.

The **Aspen Loop**, **Sabino Dawn** and **Aspen Draw Trails** are easy, cool walks through thick stands of pine, aspen and fir. See page 44. The hikes to the **Summit Crags** are covered in the next section, on page 47.

Soldier Trail, Milepost 1.4 (5.2 miles roundtrip; beginning elevation 3200', ending elevation 4800', elevation gain=1600'; allow three hours roundtrip). Since it is low on the mountain, this hike can be done in the morning in winter when it is often too cold farther up the mountain. Conversely, do not try this in the summer past 9:00 am.

The trail follows an abandoned road used to build a power line to the old **Federal Prison Camp** at the end of the hike. Inmates from the camp built the Mount Lemmon Highway in the 1930's. Today the trail is popular with hikers who want a moderate workout. The van from Canyon Ranch, a world famous health spa, can often be seen parked here as its wealthy inmates ply the trail with the rest of us.

Green Mountain Trail, Milepost 17.4, San Pedro Vista (4.2 miles roundtrip; beginning elevation 7300', ending elevation 6950', elevation gain=350'; allow two hours roundtrip). Tracking along the north slope of the mountain the Green Mountain Trail winds through beautiful pine country; cool in the summer and cold in the winter.

Follow the trail from the right side of the parking lot at **San Pedro Vista**. The trail drops gradually and in 0.3 mile you will encounter a trail junction with the recently recleared **Brush Corral Trail**. Avoid this unless you have lots of time, energy and water. You could get in serious trouble exploring this area unless you are very well prepared.

Continue along the mountainside, climbing steadily until **Maverick Spring Trail Junction** is encountered. The spring is located 4/10th mile away and is well worth seeing. From the junction the Green Mountain Trail continues climbing to Bear Saddle at 6900' on

Facing Page: Catalina Highway near Geology Vista with Tucson and Kitt Peak in the background.

the crest of the Catalinas. You have come 2.1 miles and this is the end of the hike as summarized above. You can continue down the trail for another 1.8 miles and come out at the General Hitchcock Picnic Area. If you do, retrace the Green Mountain Trail back to San Pedro Vista or arrange a car shuttle. The walk back up the highway is not recommended as it will be noisy and unpleasant.

Butterfly Trail (to Novio Spring), Milepost 19.8, Palisades Ranger Station, (6.4 miles roundtrip; beginning elevation 7950', ending elevation 6700', elevation gain=1260'; allow 3.5 hours roundtrip). This hike offers a variety of vegetation and includes thick stands of huge **ponderosa pines**. There are often bright splashes of color from penstemon, Indian paintbrush, and hedgehog cactus blooms.

Start next the big water tank across the road from the **Palisades Ranger Station** (7950') and take the Mt. Bigelow Trail uphill 1/2 mile to the saddle between **Kellogg Mt.** and **Mt. Bigelow** (8300') where you will pick up the Butterfly Trail; for the next two miles the trail loses elevation to the the junction with the Davis Trail (7150'); continue downhill another 0.7 mile to Novio Spring--a lush, cool spot. Turn back here for the 6.4 mile round trip.

Many people continue on the Butterfly Trail past Novio Spring reemerging on the highway at **Soldier Camp** (7700'). Most folks who do this arrange to leave one car at each end of the trail. The walk back down the road to the Palisades Ranger Station is not recommended.

If you decide to continue on to Soldier Camp, the length of the hike is 5.7 miles and the elevation gain is 1,000'.

𝕌𝕣𝕀𝔻𝕌𝕣𝕀𝔻𝕌𝕣𝕀𝔻𝕌𝕣 THE SUMMIT CRAGS

Area of Town: Northwest.

Map Reference: See the hiking map on page 43.

Phone Number: 602-749-8700 (Santa Catalina Ranger District)

Directions: Take Grant or Speedway east to Tanque Verde. Continue on Tanque Verde to the Catalina Highway sign, then go left and follow the road for 30 miles as it winds up the mountain. Fill up with gas before you go, <u>there is no gas at the top of Mount Lemmon</u>.

Best Time of Year: Anytime the road is open, it is especially beautiful if there is snow; occasionally you can even cross country ski out to the crags.

Best Time of Day: It will be pretty cold in the morning at this elevation in the winter.

Hours: 24 hours.

Rules: Pets on leash; the crags, or some of them, may be closed for peregrine falcon nesting season in the spring. If so, they will be posted.

Fees: None.

Facilities: None.

Nearby Places of Interest: Mount Lemmon Ski Valley; Summerhaven; Marshall Gulch.

Comments:

The Summit Crags are several huge granite outcroppings on the northwest side of Mount Lemmon which make excellent view points. The driving directions are the same for each. Just keep going on the road past the ski area and through the open gate to the top. Park before the entrance for the observatory (not open to the public) and then look for a dirt road with a gate going down the hill to the west (left). All of the rocks can be reached with a 30 to 40 minute walk.

Stay off these rocks if there is a thunderstorm anywhere in the vicinity -- they get hit regularly by lightning.

Lemmon Rock has the Forest Service lookout on it and is the easiest destination. Just follow the signs down the road and out to the left, you can't miss it. From here you will be able to see the other crags discussed below.

Rappel Rock. Go right instead of left to Lemmon Rock when you reach the intersection with the road which runs along the side of the mountain. Keep going a few hundred yards and just past where the road goes by a tin shed (protecting the Quartzite Spring) head downhill to Rappel Rock. The climb to the top can be a little daring but no special equipment is needed, except if you fall, then you'll wish you had been roped.

Next along the road are **The Ravens**, a spectacular series of granite spires stacked against each other. To get there keep going past the turn off for Rappel Rock and you will soon see the spires through the trees on the left. A distinct path traverses out the short saddle connecting the Ravens to the Mount Lemmon massif. If you are agile you can scramble up on the first spire to get a look around. The others take technical know-how and equipment to ascend.

To reach the **Fortress,** continue along the road past the Ravens for a couple of hundred feet up a slight hill to an obvious path which leads to the rock. The scramble to the top of the rock is pretty easy.

Mt. Lemmon Ski Valley

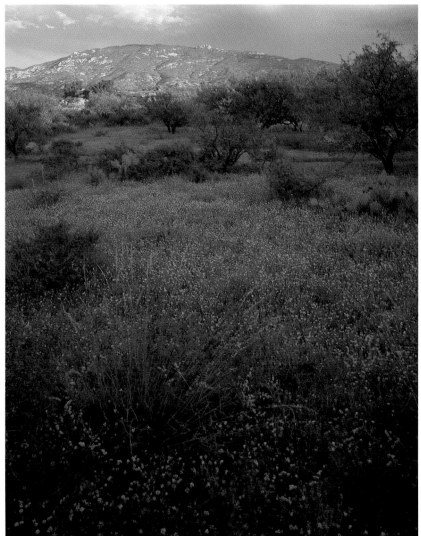

The Rincon Mountains, © *Randy Prentice*

RINCON MOUNTAINS

Area of Town: East.

Map Reference: E, F, 12-13; see also map on page16.

Phone Number: 602-296-8576 Saguaro National Monument (East).

Directions: Take Broadway or Speedway east to Houghton Road and go right to Old Spanish Trail and follow it to the Visitors Center of the Saguaro National Monument (East).

Best Time of Year: All year, but avoid mid-day in the summer unless you plan to stay in the car for an air-conditioned cruise of the loop road.

Best Time of Day: Early and late for the good light but perhaps mid-day if the weather is frigid.

Hours: The mountains are open for business 24 hours but the Cactus Forest Drive in Saguaro National Monument (East) is only open from 7:00 am to 7:00 pm. The Visitors Center is open from 8:00 am to 5:00 pm.

Rules: No pets on the trails in Saguaro National Monument.

Fees: One vehicle is $4.00; bikes and buses pay $2.00 per person; an annual pass for the Monument only is $10.00; Golden Access pass good at all National Parks and Monuments is $25.00; Golden Age Pass Holders free.

Facilities: Restrooms; picnic areas but no camping.

Nearby Places of Interest: Follow Old Spanish Trail south a few miles to Colossal Cave which has a regular tour.

Comments:

This massive range is not easily visited. There is no road into the range and even the trail approaches tend to be long. Probably the best way to see these mountains if you don't have the time or inclination for a long walk, is to drive the loop road in Saguaro National Monument. The views of the Rincons are excellent and the monument has its share of attractions, including good nature trails and picnic areas. There are also great view points on the east side of the loop to watch the **sunset**.

Another possibility to see the Rincons from another direction (but also at a distance) is to drive out the Redington Pass Rd. To get to it, take Tanque Verde east until it turns into Redington Pass Rd. It is rugged and dusty but does allow good views of the north slope of the Rincons and some very typical Arizona cattle country. If you look around you will find some picturesque corrals and windmills.

If you want to get into the foothills before the loop road opens at 7:00 am, you can hike in on the **Douglas Spring Trail** at the end of Speedway or the **Cactus Forest Trail** which starts near the end of Broadway. The Douglas Spring Trail reaches the Douglas Spring campground in 5.9 miles and eventually leads to the top of the mountains. You can do as much as you are comfortable with and then turn back. The Cactus Forest Trail heads back toward the Visitors Center and gives good access to that part of the monument.

To actually get up into the Rincons aways try the **Tanque Verde Ridge Trail** which starts near the Javelina Picnic area off the loop road in the Monument. The hike to **Juniper Basin** is 6.9 miles and takes 6 or 7 hours round trip. The hike to the top of the range is a lot farther. But there are terrific views a mile up the trail and you can just turn back when you are tired.

ᛗᛖᛚᚱᛗᛖᛚᚱᛗᛖᛚᚱ TUCSON MOUNTAINS

Area of Town: West.
Map Reference: D, E 3; see also map pages 54-55.
Phone Number: 602-740-2690 (Pima County Parks & Recreation Department).
Directions: Take Speedway Blvd. west past I-10 and it will turn into Gates Pass Rd. as it ascends into the Tucson Mountains.
Best Time of Year: This is the hottest spot around Tucson in the summer; the black rock seems to generate its own heat. On the other hand it is often toasty in the **winter** when it is too cool to hike elsewhere.
Best Time of Day: Mid-day in the winter, early and late when it is warmer.
Hours: 7:00 am to 10:00 pm.
Rules: Pets on leash; no alcohol.
Fees: None, except for camping.
Facilities: Camping; picnicking; restrooms.
Nearby Places of Interest: Arizona-Sonora Desert Museum; Old Tucson.

Comments:

Driving

D riving through Gates Pass gives a good close-up view of these rugged mountains. The road starts as Speedway Blvd. but the name changes to **Gates Pass Road** as it starts to wind up into the Tucson Mountains. The canyon closes in on the road as it rises toward the pass. Saguaros range down the hillsides to road's edge, along with ocotilla and a variety of cholla.

At the pass there is a **picnic area** where a stop may be made to enjoy the view into the Avra Valley to the west. There is also a nice little "pocket" view of Tucson to the east. After the picnic area the road makes a sharp left and heads steeply downhill, clinging perilously to the mountain side. The passengers on the right side get a death-defying view of space, the car is too close to the road's edge to even see it. Nary a guardrail is in sight, partner. No trailers!

After reaching Kinney Rd. turn right and then left on the **McCain Loop Rd**. for an excellent opportunity to view the vast bajadas spreading into the Avra Valley. The saguaro forest here is excellent and there are plenty of places to pull off and look around.

If you continue on Kinney Rd. past the **Saguaro National Monument visitors center** about a mile and a half you will see the right turn for the **Bajada Loop Drive**, a well maintained dirt road through the north foothills of the Tucson Mountains. If you take the turn off the loop signed for the **Sendero Esperanza Picnic Area** this is **Golden Gate Rd**. which can be followed to **Picture Rocks Rd**. A right turn on Picture Rocks Rd. will take you back to Tucson.

A more **urban view** of the Tucson Mountains and the many homes, both noble and awful, which have been built there, can be had by driving along **Camino del Oeste** (Road of the West). Turn right (north) onto Camino de Oeste from Gates Pass Rd./Speedway Blvd. about three miles west of I-10. After two and a half miles of ups and downs you will encounter Sweetwater Drive which can be taken to Silverbell Rd.; a right turn will lead back to Speedway.

The heart of the Tucson Mountains has been penetrated by home building at **Trails End Road**. Take the first road west (left) off Camino de Oeste about a half mile north of Speedway. The subdivision at the end is private but the views on the road are very good.

"A" Mountain (officially Sentinel Peak) is one of the best view spots in Tucson. The little mountain perches over the downtown area and has a road to the top. The road is open from 7:00 am to 10:00 pm, which is too bad because it would make a great place to see the sunrise. It is a great place to see the sunset although you can not see much of the sun actually going down because the view is cut off by the rest of the Tucson Mountains. Nonetheless, the views of the sunset glow on the valley and especially on the Santa Catalina Mountains are superb.

To get to "A" Mountain take Congress St. west from downtown, or the I-10 exit for a few blocks and make a left on Cuesta Ave. where Congress goes right. Follow Cuesta a short way and it turns into Sentinel Peak Rd. which is followed to the top.

Facing Page: Moonrise over Tucson, ©*Randy Prentice*

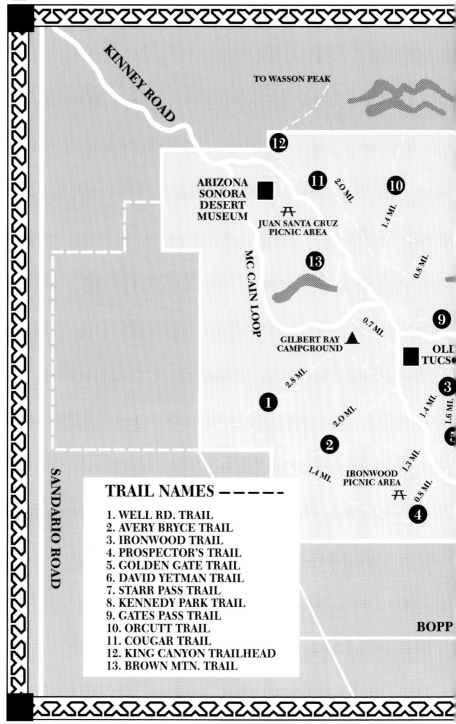

TO WASSON PEAK

⑫

ARIZONA SONORA DESERT MUSEUM

⑪ 2.0 MI.

⑩ 1.4 MI.

JUAN SANTA CRUZ PICNIC AREA

0.8 MI.

KINNEY ROAD

MC CAIN LOOP

⑬

⑨

0.7 MI.

GILBERT RAY CAMPGROUND

OLI TUCS

2.8 MI.

③

① 1.4 MI.

1.6 MI.

2.0 MI.

②

1.3 MI.

1.4 MI.

IRONWOOD PICNIC AREA

0.8 MI.

④

SANDARIO ROAD

BOPP

TRAIL NAMES – – – – –

1. WELL RD. TRAIL
2. AVERY BRYCE TRAIL
3. IRONWOOD TRAIL
4. PROSPECTOR'S TRAIL
5. GOLDEN GATE TRAIL
6. DAVID YETMAN TRAIL
7. STARR PASS TRAIL
8. KENNEDY PARK TRAIL
9. GATES PASS TRAIL
10. ORCUTT TRAIL
11. COUGAR TRAIL
12. KING CANYON TRAILHEAD
13. BROWN MTN. TRAIL

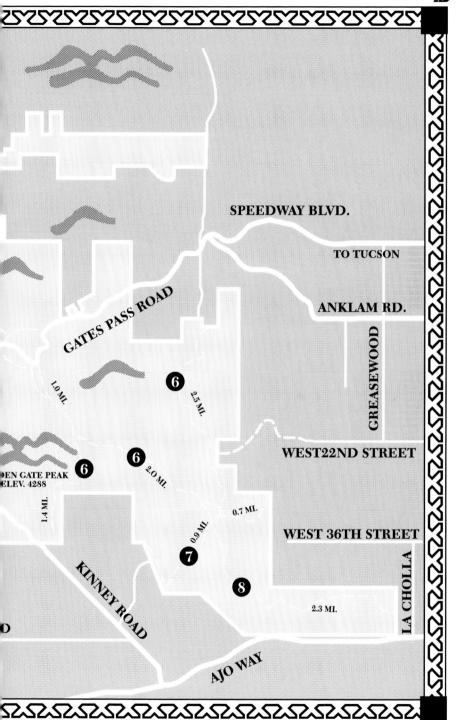

SPEEDWAY BLVD.

TO TUCSON

ANKLAM RD.

GATES PASS ROAD

GREASEWOOD

1.0 MI.

6 2.5 MI.

WEST22ND STREET

6 6 2.0 MI.

EN GATE PEAK
ELEV. 4288

1.4 MI.

0.7 MI.

WEST 36TH STREET

0.9 MI.

7

8

LA CHOLLA

2.3 MI.

KINNEY ROAD

AJO WAY

Hiking

The Tucson Mountains are much richer in flora and fauna than it appears just driving by. A good **moderate hike** to explore the range is the **King Canyon Trail**. The trailhead is located just across the road from the entrance to the Arizona-Sonora Desert Museum. It is 3.5 miles to the junction with the Hugh Norris Trail and you will gain 1800 feet in elevation. Allow 2 hours up and 1 1/2 hours to return.

Of course there is no rule saying you have to hike all the way up to the ridge; in 20 minutes you will be at the **Mam-a-gah Picnic Area** at the bottom of the wash. There is often running water here and plenty of flowers. Indeed this is the only permanent source of water in the Tucson Mountains. If you head downstream you will encounter extensive petroglyphs. See page 102.

A classic Tucson Mountain hike of **moderate difficulty** is **Sendero Esperanza Trail to Wasson Peak** (4,687'), the highest point in the range. A full description of this hike is given on page 24.

The hike is gradual, covering 3.2 miles each way with an elevation gain of 1900 feet. Allow two hours each way. There are grand views all the way and often there will be wildflowers as well. Be sure to take two quarts of water each and remember it can be cool at the top.

A really nice **easy hike** in the northern foothills of the Tucsons is the

Valley View Overlook Trail. Located off the Bajada Loop Drive it is fairly level and covers about one mile round trip. See map on page 12. Allow about 45 minutes round trip. Handsome granite rock formations top the ridge where the trail ends. The desert is very open here and there are fine cactus specimens of many kinds. The views are excellent and this makes a terrific place to see the **sunset**.

MADERA CANYON

Area Of Town: 35 miles south.
Map Reference: X 5.
Phone Number: 602-281-2296 (Nogales Ranger Station).
Directions: Take I-10 to I-19 about 30 miles south and get off at Continental Rd. (Exit 63)/ Follow Continental Rd. east and then follow the signs to the canyon.
Best Time Of Year: All year.
Best Time Of Day: Anytime, but the birds may be easier to spot early in the morning before it gets crowded.
Hours: 24 Hours.
Rules: Pets on leash.
Fees: None.
Facilities: Restrooms; a few camping spots; good picnic facilities; Santa Rita lodge, 4 cabins, 8 rooms 602-625-8746.
Nearby Places Of Interest: Titan Missile Museum, Green Valley; Tubac; Tumacacori National Monument.

Comments:

This oak-forested canyon has been a favorite with everyone who has visited since the days of the Spaniards. The road ends at 5,000 feet where there are good picnic facilities and numerous trailheads.

Approaching the canyon from the valley, the road winds through rolling grassland included in the **Santa Rita Experimental Range**. The **Proctor Parking Area** at the entrance to the canyon, and the **Whitehorse Picnic Area**, there is access to the **nature trails** which are accessible to wheelchairs.

The **Madera trailhead and Picnic Area** is the start of the **Bog Spring Trail**, an easy, recommendable hike.

At the end of the road the trailheads for 9,453-foot **Mt. Wrightson** or **"Old Baldy"** are marked. These hikes gain over 4,000 feet and will take several hours each way. Take at least 2 liters of water per person and something warm to wear at the top because it may be cold and windy, even in warmer weather. The views are worth the hike but it is a strenuous affair. The choice of trails to the top are the **"Super Trail"** which is longer (14.4 miles roundtrip) but more gradual, or the steeper but shorter (10 miles roundtrip) **"Old Baldy Trail"**.

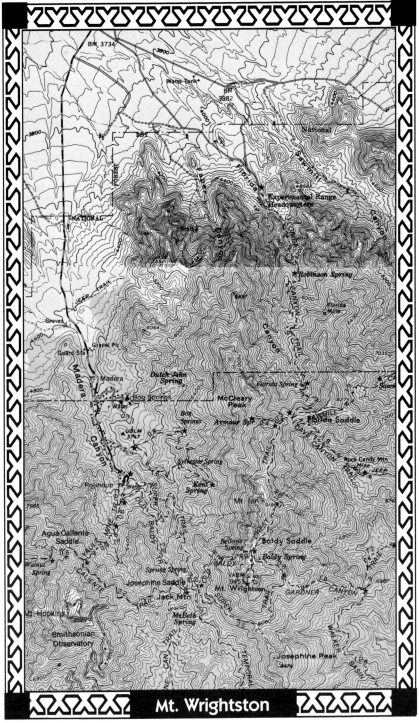

Mt. Wrightston

There are many waterfalls around Tucson when the winter or summer storms fill the canyons. Some are serene little fountains feeding small pools and some are thundering cataracts, frightening with their enormous energy constricted into tight canyons.

Safety. Please remember that many people have been injured or killed sightseeing around these waterfalls. Twenty seven people have died at **Tanque Verde Falls** since 1971 and many more have been injured. With the explicit warnings posted you wonder how it happens. Well, the answer is often a combination of the youthful surety that "It can't happen to me" and the water-polished rock which has the traction of a banana peel. This is especially true with bare feet. Swimmers have also been drowned when they were sucked under and held by the force of tons of water coming over the falls. Alcohol has also played a part in many of the accidents.

Seven Falls is probably the most visited of the waterfalls, although it requires a hike of an hour or so to get there. This is a lot **safer** than Tanque Verde Falls and there are great spots for sun bathing.

When they are running at full tilt **Tanque Verde Falls** are incredible. The noise and vibration filling the narrow granite canyon is awesome. The road is unpaved, dusty and bumpy but the hike in is short.

Seven Cataracts fall into Upper Bear Canyon. They are directly across from the pullout at milepost 9.1 of the Catalina Highway. They are a bear to get to as you must bushwhack down the canyon side without a trail. The scramble back up is loose, steep and difficult. Do not attempt this unless you are really committed. Once there though, you can enjoy the grottos formed around the bottom of each cataract with huge Arizona cypress trees dominating the scene.

Photo Tips. The shadows may make the use of a warming filter like an 81A worthwhile. For that "misty" look to the water, use a tripod and a shutter speed of 1/8th or less.

SEVEN FALLS

Area of Town: Northeast.

Map Reference: See map on page 31.

Phone Number: 602-749-8700 (Santa Catalina Ranger District); 749-2861 (Shuttle Bus Information)

Directions: From the foothills take Sunrise Rd. or River Rd. east to Sabino Canyon Rd., turn left and then right at the Visitors Center. From midtown take Speedway or Grant Rd. east to Wilmot and turn left. Wilmot turns into Tanque Verde Rd. as it turns east. Continue east for about one mile then turn left on Sabino Canyon Rd. and follow it to the Visitors Center. Once there you can walk to the trailhead (allow 45 minutes additional) or take the tram which runs on the hour. If you decide to walk, take the big wide path that leads out of the east end of the Visitors Center parking lot to the road and then follow the road to the trail head. The trail itself takes about an hour to walk and it was badly damaged by the flood of 1993 so it is a little difficult to follow in spots. Look for cairns (little piles of rock) placed to mark the way.

Best Time of Year: It will be hard to enjoy this attraction in the heat of the summer.

Best Time of Day: Early or late in the day is best for viewing and picture taking. Mid-day in the winter should be warm enough if the sun is out.

Hours: 24 Hours; tram runs from 9:00 am to 4:00 pm on the hour to Lower Bear Canyon.

Rules: No pets.

Fees: None; tram is $3.00 for adults & $1.25 for children.

Facilities: Drinking water, restrooms, tram, picnic areas, Visitors Center.

Nearby Places of Interest: You pass Lower Sabino Canyon when you are tramming or walking to the trail head. The pond there makes a nice stop and offers a nice reflecting spot for photographs. Upper Sabino Canyon is also available if you find you have a lot of energy left.

Comments:

This is a very popular spot and if the weather is warm there will be a lot of sunbathers. The falls are very accessible (once you have done the hike in) and the pools under them make great resting spots. Be careful about scrambling up to the upper falls as the rock is slippery. You cannot drink the water from the creek so take plenty, especially if it is warm.

Facing Page: Seven Falls, © Peter Noebels

TANQUE VERDE FALLS

Area of Town: East.

Map Reference: D 12.

Phone Number: 602-749-8700 (Santa Catalina Ranger District)

Directions: From midtown drive east on Speedway or Grant to Wilmot Rd. and turn left. Follow Wilmot as it curves east and turns into Tanque Verde Rd. Continue east past the turnoff for the Catalina Highway. Beyond here Tanque Verde becomes Redington Rd. Follow Redington Rd. for 7.5 miles and the pavement runs out. The road can be pretty bumpy but it is passable to the falls. In less than a mile there is a sign on the right for the trail to **Lower Tanque Verde Falls** and on the left there is a parking lot.

For Upper Tanque Verde Falls continue up the road for another 3/4 mile and there is a sign for the trail on the right. There is no parking lot but there are a number of pullouts.

Best Time of Year: September to November and March to May; but on a fine day it is always entertaining if there has been heavy precipitation or snow melt.

Best Time of Day: Early and late for the light. In warm weather you may want to avoid the heat of mid-day and late afternoon. In cooler weather consider letting it warm up a bit before starting out, as the canyon will be shaded to some extent and can be cold.

Hours: 24 Hours.

Rules: Pets on leash.

Fees: None.

Facilities: None.

Nearby Places of Interest: If the Redington Road has been graded recently it makes a good drive to see some typical Arizona cattle country, and get good views of the north side of the Rincon Mountains. There also is good **mountain biking** in this area.

Comments:

Lower **Tanque Verde Falls Trail** was built by the Southern Arizona Rescue Association. About a half mile long and very well constructed and gradual, it makes their job easier on their regular trips to this area.

This area is not a wilderness experience, unless you mean the kind they show in the beer commercials. The main attraction here is sunbathing. There are nice pools and spectacular waterfalls. Hiking/scrambling about 20 or 30 minutes upstream will get you to the big falls. There is a lot of slippery rock, so be careful and don't become a statistic. Before you get to

Facing Page: Creek below Lower Tanque Verde Falls

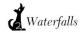

the big falls there is a smaller one to be bypassed or climbed. I'd recommend you bypass it on the right via the trail on the canyon side. You will note the amazingly small helipad constructed on a tiny outcropping of rock. This is for taking the accident victims out. **Do not** try to climb above the big falls.

Not to harp on it, but there is another danger of which you should be aware. If it is raining in the mountains there can be a flash flood down this drainage even though it is not raining at the falls. Several years ago five people were swept to their deaths by a wall of water which caught them as they were assisting or spectating in the helicopter rescue of a person who had been injured in a fall.

Upper Tanque Verde Falls Trail leads to an area with a handsome sculpted falls at the base of the trail. If you continue downstream you will encounter the top of the big falls. But from the top you really can't see anything and the temptation is to try to get down a little further to get a better view. **THIS IS A BIG MISTAKE !** The sign above the falls says "Many have died here" and that's the truth. In fact, a number have died here since that sign was erected in 1981. If you want to see the falls, come up from the lower end and still be extremely careful.

SEVEN CATARACTS

Area of Town: Northeast.

Map Reference: B 12; see also map on page 39.

Phone Number: 602-749-8700 (Santa Catalina Ranger District).

Directions: Take Grant Rd. or Speedway Blvd. to Tanque Verde Rd. to the Catalina Highway then go left and follow the road as it winds up the mountain.

Once on the Catalina Highway you will navigate by the mileposts. At milepost 9.1 there is a large pullout on the left just before the road heads east (right) into Upper Bear Canyon. Park here and look directly across the canyon.

Best Time of Year: Willow Canyon, which is the source of the Seven Cataracts, is not a big drainage. As a result the runoff which produces the cataracts occurs only when there is heavy rain or snow in the drainage above. Sometime in the late winter or early spring there will be enough precipitation combined with snow melt to produce impressive falls. Also, after a series of summer thunderstorms there can be enough runoff to produce a good show. The bad news is that you cannot predict when there will be a lot of water. The good news is that you can see from the car whether the cataracts are flowing so you won't waste a vicious approach in and out of the canyon to find out.

Best Time of Day: Since these falls face south, mid or late day will usually be better. But, if it is hot, remember that the hike back up to the car from the canyon bottom is strenuous.

Hours: 24 Hours.

Rules: Pets on leash.

Fees: None.

Facilities: None, but there are restrooms and picnic facilities in Bear Canyon just a few minutes up the road.

Nearby Places of Interest: Windy Point.

Comments:

Unless you are prepared for a stiff hike, this is not for you. It takes about 45 minutes each way to reach the falls, there is no trail and the canyon side is loose and steep.

The cataracts can be seen from the road, but only with binoculars are they impressive.

If you are committed enough to do the hike, you will be entranced by the unique setting at the pools under the roaring falls. The Arizona cypress are very similar in appearance to cedar trees and tower above the pools, lending a gracious symmetry to the rugged canyon. The cataracts tumble 1,200 feet down **Willow Canyon** as it turns south and joins Upper Bear Canyon.

To a visitor fresh from a greener place, the Tucson landscape can look bleak, particularly in mid-day light. More time in the desert will dispel this impression for many people. Oldtime Tucsonans kind of hibernate during the mid-day; they know the desert is at its best early and late in the day.

Morning and afternoon light turns many desert plants into backlit magic. Cactis like **teddy bear cholla** glow when the sun's rays bend around the thousands of spines. Some cactus like the **saguaro** and **organ pipe** give a red cast to the glow to further liven things up. Even the **creosote bush** will light up in oblique light, especially when they are covered with their fuzzy little pods late in the spring.

Many people are surprised by the outrageous flower shows the cactus put on. The normally prosaic **prickly pear** cacti put out brilliant yellow blossoms by the dozen. Stick-like **staghorn** cactus sport a host of smallish multi-hued flowers. In May the saguaros are topped with the most wonderful creamy white blossoms.

In April the hillsides are painted yellow with blooming **brittlebush**. In May the entire Tucson area turns bright yellow as the palo verde trees bloom. Depending on the year, the desert floor may be carpeted with a variety of **poppies**, **lupines**, **owl clover** or other wildflowers. A **calendar** of when different plants bloom is contained in Appendix Five.

Although Tucson's seasons are different than elsewhere, they are well defined to those who have lived here awhile. There is even a bit of fall color when the leaves change on the **cottonwood trees** in the Rillito River and Sabino Canyon. For those who journey up Mount Lemmon in late October, there is a fantastic display of gold in the **aspen groves** around Marshall Gulch. Combined with the red maples in the draws around Summerhaven and in Bear Wallow occasionally, the total effect is definitely fall foliage.

If you drive around in desert areas, especially early or late in the day, you are going to see many desert critters. Common varieties like **coyotes, quail, rabbits, deer, lizards, rattlesnakes, javelina** and **ground squirrels** can be seen virtually everyday. Other species like the **mountain lions, bears, foxes,** and **eagles** are not often sighted. But still, the bear on Mount Lemmon are seen occasionally as are **bobcats** and **gila monsters**. Even the shy **desert bighorn sheep** are sometimes spotted near the upscale neighborhoods adjoining Coronado National Forest.

But, you don't have to rely on chance to see a full array of Sonoran desert wildlife. Tucson is home to the finest manmade habitat for desert

Facing Page: Soaptree yucca pods, Santa Catalina Mountains

wildlife in the world. The **Arizona-Sonora Desert Museum** presents an unparalleled opportunity to see desert wildlife in natural settings, with a excellent chance to get a good photograph. <u>DON'T MISS IT !</u> Every representative animal is featured from prairie dogs to bears and from hummingbirds to eagles. The rare Mexican wolf is a resident as well as a variety of exotic cats native to the Sonoran desert.

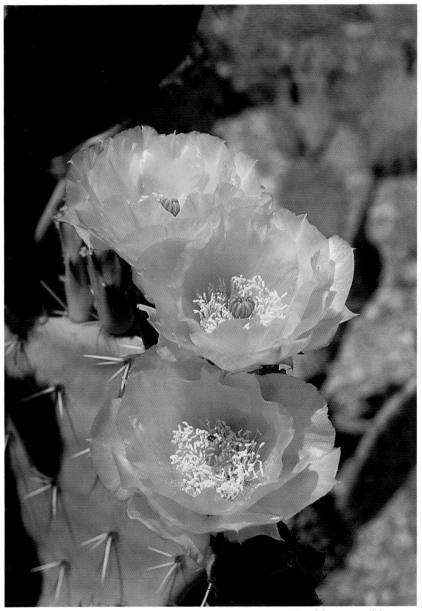

Prickley pear blossoms

Cactus and Other Native Plants

Everywhere you look in Tucson there are cacti. In this section you will be pointed toward those places where there are especially fine specimens and where they are massed for the most effect for viewing and photographing.

One of the most convenient places to see cacti is the **Saguaro National Monument (East)**. The eight-mile loop drive is paved and has convenient pullouts. The paved 1/4 mile **Desert Ecology Trail** is accessible to wheelchairs. Access to much of **Saguaro National Monument (West)** is also easy and features the finest saguaro forest in the world.

Tucson Mountain Park covers an enormous section of rugged mountains and contains fine stands of saguaros and many other cacti. Especially impressive are the thick stands of teddy bear cholla below Gates Pass.

The **Arizona-Sonora Desert Museum** has a great variety of cacti which are conveniently identified. It also sits in a wonderful forest of saguaro and has grand views into the valley.

Tohono Chul Park is located in the heart of rapidly expanding northwest Tucson. It preserves a 40-acre parcel of desert and has good interpretive aids to explain the desert and its plants. The cactus shop offers a close up view of many fine small cacti which are for sale. This is a great place to have lunch in the charming Tea Room.

Tanque Verde Greenhouses located on Redington Rd. east of town has an extraordinary collection of exotic cactus from the desert southwest and around the world. You can take a picture of a cacti or take it home.

Catalina State Park is included because the saguaro habitat is markedly different from the other areas. On the south facing slopes of the small canyons coming out of the Santa Catalina Mountains grow lush stands of huge saguaros.

Photo Tips: Shooting pictures of cacti at mid-day can produce disappointing results. The colors, except the flowers, are not vivid and are easily washed out in the sun. Use the **softer light** of early morning or late afternoon to capture the subtle tones of the plants. Shooting from a position where the sun is coming through the spines and **backlighting** the subject will make a dramatic photograph. You may need to adjust the exposure either manually or by using a built-in backlight feature if your camera has one. **Close-up** or **macro** pictures also can be striking when clusters of spines or flowers are highlighted.

SAGUARO NATIONAL MONUMENT (East)

Area of Town: East.

Map Reference: E 11; see also map on page 16.

Phone Number: 602-296-8576 (National Park Service).

Directions: Take Broadway or Speedway east to Houghton Road, turn right and go on to **Old Spanish Trail** and turn left. Follow it to the Visitors Center of the Saguaro National Monument (East).

Best Time of Year: All year but most cacti bloom in spring and it will be hot after 9:00 a.m. during the summer.

Best Time of Day: Early and late except when it is cold during the winter.

Hours: The mountains are open for business 24 hours but the Cactus Forest Drive in Saguaro National Monument (East) is only open from 7:00 am to 7:00 pm. As long as you are on the loop drive by 7:00 pm you can stay until dark. The Visitors Center is open from 8:00 am to 5:00 pm.

Rules: No pets on the trails in Saguaro National Monument.

Fees: One vehicle is $4.00; bikes and buses pay $2.00 per person; an annual pass for the Monument only is $10.00; Golden Access pass good at all National Parks and Monuments is $25.00; Golden Age Pass holders free.

Facilities: Visitors Center; picnic areas; drinking water and restrooms.

Nearby Places of Interest: Tanque Verde Greenhouse is located north of the Monument at 10810 Tanque Verde Rd.. Follow Old Spanish Trail south to Colossal Cave which has a regular tour.

Comments:

Some people do not see Tucson as a desert because they come expecting to see sand dunes like the Sahara and instead see a lush (for a desert) landscape. The Cactus Forest loop road in the east unit of Saguaro National Monument passes through some of the thickest of Sonoran desert vegetation. Yes, there are saguaros and other varieties of cactus in abundance, but there are also a lot of grasses and trees which soften the hillsides. This unit of the monument is far different than the more stark desert appearance of the west unit located in the Tucson Mountains.

Drive the 8-mile Cactus Forest Drive; there are plenty of opportunities to stop and stroll through the desert. This also makes a fine bicycle ride if you are so inclined and can handle the gently rolling hills, including one called "heartbreak hill" by the joggers.

If you go early or stay late you may have an opportunity to watch the coyotes making their rounds. Many desert critters don't seem to mind people in cars and often you can get quite close. If you want more privacy hike in on one of the trails that start from the end of Speedway; they are well marked.

Besides some fine specimens of giant saguaro (although not as many as the west unit) and the ubiquitous prickly pear, there are huge chain and staghorn cholla. All the cacti put out colorful flowers at some time in the spring. See Appendix Five for a calendar of when plants bloom in the desert.

Among the trees, **foothills palo verde** and **mesquite** predominate. The palo verdes put on an incredible show in April each year as they turn the hillsides gold with their blossoms. The **ironwood trees** have a subtle purple blossom in May or June.

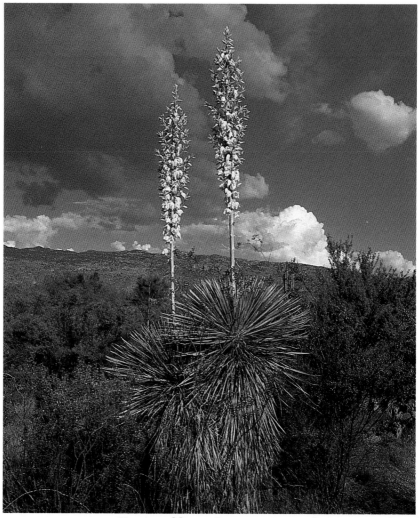

Yucca in bloom, Saguaro National Monument (East)

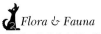

SAGUARO NATIONAL MONUMENT (West)

Area of Town: West.

Map Reference: D 2; see also map page 12.

Phone Number: 602-883-6366 (National Park Service).

Directions: From the north side of town take Ina Rd. west past I-10 until it ends. Then go left on Wade Rd. which shortly turns into Picture Rock Rd. and keep going almost seven miles to the stop sign at Sandario Rd. Take a left and go about 3.6 miles to Kinney Rd. and go left. In about 1.8 miles you'll come to the Visitors Center.

If you are prepared for a long, slow dirt road ride you can take the "short cut" by going left on **Golden Gate Road**, about two miles after you enter the monument on Picture Rocks Rd. This eventually intersects with Sandario Rd. where you make a left and then another left on Kinney Rd. a short ways later, arriving at the Visitors Center in 2.5 miles. From midtown go over Gates Pass to the stop sign at Kinney Rd. Take a right and go about 4.8 twisting and beautiful miles to the Visitors Center.

From the south side of town take Ajo Way (Hwy 86) to Kinney Rd., go right on Kinney for about seven miles to the Visitors Center.

Best Time of Year: All year, but the cacti mostly bloom in spring and it will be hot after 9:00 am during the summer.

Best Time of Day: Early and late except when it is cold during the winter.

Hours: 24 Hours.

Rules: No pets on trails; no driving off-road.

Fees: None.

Facilities: Visitors Center; picnic areas; drinking water and rest rooms.

Nearby Places of Interest: Gates Pass; Old Tucson; Arizona-Sonora Desert Museum.

Comments:

Wow! Maybe it's the dirt roads, but one feels more "in" the desert in the West unit of Saguaro National Monument. Also, it is undeniable that the stands of saguaros here are denser than in the East unit. There are great views into the Avra Valley from most of the Monument and wonderful trails and picnic areas with stone buildings built by the CCC in the 1930's.

The **Red Hills Information Center** is staffed with helpful rangers to answer your questions. It also has an excellent small book shop specializing in the flora and fauna of the monument.

Hiking the **Hugh Norris Trail**, the **Valley View Trail** or just stopping by the side of the road will give you a fine opportunity to see majestic stands of saguaros. The scene is especially impressive where they range up the rugged hillsides next to the Hugh Norris Trail and the **Ezkiminzin Picnic Area** on the **Bajada Loop Road**.

While other cacti like staghorn, barrel, chain cholla and hedgehog are well represented here, the main attraction is the giant saguaro. Both the Red Hills Information Center and the interpretative trails are good sources of additional information about this fascinating plant.

Be sure to visit the **wildlife viewpoint** near the water hole just up the road from the Red Hills Information Center. Also, the **Desert Discovery Nature Trail** has good interpretive signs explaining the desert environment. Finally, don't leave without taking the short walk from the Signal Hill Picnic area to see the outstanding **petroglyphs** on **Signal Hill**.

Saguaro in bloom

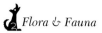

TUCSON MOUNTAIN PARK

Area of Town: West.

Map Reference: D, E 3; see map on pages 54-55.

Phone Number: 602-740-2690 (Pima County Parks).

Directions: This is a big park with accesses from every direction. For the **David Yetman trailhead** discussed in the comments section follow Speedway west past I-10 as it turns to Gates Pass Rd. and go through the pass and down the mountain on the other side. Park in the pullout on the left at the hairpin turn.

Best Time of Year: All year, but avoid midday in the summer.

Best Time of Day: Early or late for viewing the teddy bear cactus; late for the sunset.

Hours: Yetman Trailhead at Gates Pass 7:00 am to dark, 8:30pm in the summer; picnic areas from 7:00 am to 8:00 pm.

Rules: Pets on leash; no firearms; no alcohol.

Fees: None, except camping in the Gilbert Ray Campground.

Facilities: Restrooms; picnic areas; camping.

Nearby Places of Interest: Old Tucson; Arizona-Sonora Desert Museum; Saguaro National Monument (West).

Comments:

Fully exploring this excellent park with its rugged mountains and lush canyons would take a long winter season with a lot of spare time. There are numerous trails and you are encouraged to strike out on your own to discover your own favorite places here.

The park is a treasure-trove of cacti and other Sonoran desert vegetation. Of particular interest are the **teddy bear cholla** growing in thick groves along the ridges. In the early morning light they are lit up by the backlight of the sun and are a marvel to see. Good stands within a reasonable walk are located just above the **David Yetman Trailhead** below Gates Pass. **Be careful!** The plants drop segments of spiny arms on the ground and they seem to "jump" right into your leg. A particularly nasty and common event is to pick one up in the toe of one shoe and then kick it into the back of your other leg as you walk. If you get a piece stuck on you, use a big comb, a pair of pliers or two sticks or stones to remove it. Be especially careful for **children** and pets. **Dogs** that are not desert smart can get in big trouble among the cholla.

Backlit teddy bear cholla

ARIZONA-SONORA DESERT MUSEUM

Area of Town: West
Map Reference: D 2.
Phone Number: 602-883-1380.

Directions: Take Speedway west past I-10. As it winds up into the Tucson Mountains it changes names to Gates Pass Rd. Follow this through the pass and down the other side to where the road intersects with Kinney Rd. at a stop sign. Go right and within two miles you will see the museum on the left. If you are towing a trailer or don't like mountain drives,

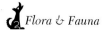

go south on I-10 and exit on Ajo Way. Then go west (right) and continue on Ajo Way to Kinney Rd. on the other side of the Tucson Mountains. At the light make a right and follow Kinney Rd. to the Desert Museum.

Best Time of Year: All year.

Best Time of Day: The early morning and late afternoon light are best for viewing and photographs. Also, the animals will be more active at those times. In the winter, when it is cool, mid-day may be just fine. It will be hot at mid-day from June to the end of September unless there have been thunderstorms to cool things off.

Hours: October through February: 8:30 am to 5:00 pm; March through September: 7:30 am to 6:00 pm.

Rules: No pets; no picnicking on museum grounds.

Fees: Adults $7.95; Children 6 to 12 years old $1.50; Children under 6 years old are free.

Facilities: Restaurant; gift shop; restrooms; wheelchair access. Camping and picnicking are not available at the museum but are available nearby in Tucson Mountain Park.

Nearby Places of Interest: Saguaro National Monument (West); Old Tucson; Gates Pass.

Comments:

The Arizona-Sonora Desert Museum is the pride of Tucson. It is a world-class setting for seeing the flora and fauna of the Sonoran desert. It gets better every year. Schedule at least two hours to see the bare bones, more to take time for photos and rest.

The Cactus Garden contains over 140 species of cacti and other Sonoran desert plants. Throughout the museum grounds are fine examples of native vegetation used to landscape the excellent animal habitats.

This is a convenient and educational way to learn about the Sonoran desert. Be sure to check the Daily Interpretive Events board at the entrance for a schedule of the day's activities and tours. Also see the demonstration garden featuring tips on desert landscaping. The life zone exhibit is a fascinating explanation of the vegetation life zones in the desert and mountains.

ᒥᕮᑐᐧᒪᕮᑐᐧᒪᕮᑐᐧᒪᕮ TOHONO CHUL PARK

Area of Town: Northwest.
Map Reference: C 6.
Phone Number: 602-575-8468 Information;
    797-1711 (Tea Room).
Directions: Take Ina Rd. west from Oracle Rd. drive west a short way to
    Paseo del Norte and turn right (north) to the signs for the park.
Best Time of Year: All year but the cacti bloom in the spring.
Best Time of Day: Early and late for the best light but midday will be fine
in the winter when the light is weaker and it is cool.
Hours: Park Grounds: 7:00 am to Sunset.
    Exhibit House 9:30 am to 5:00 pm—Monday thru Saturday, 11:00 am
    to 5:00 pm—Sundays. Tea Room: 8:00 am to 5:00 pm
Rules: No pets.
Fees: Suggested donation $2.00.
Facilities: Restaurant, restrooms, gift shop.
Nearby Places of Interest: Pima Canyon; Catalina State Park.

Comments:

This park is a jewel. Almost forty acres of desert left in the middle of the
city, it is a surprising oasis. There are walks through typical desert
settings with good interpretive material. The demonstration gardens are
beautiful and instructive.

The **Tea Room restaurant** in the old house is first class. There are
often interesting **art or crafts shows** in the **Exhibit House**. The **Park
Greenhouse** has an excellent display of native and arid land plants for
sale. This is a good place to get close-up pictures of exotic blooming cactus.

ᒪᕮᑐᐧᒪᕮ TUCSON BOTANICAL GARDENS

Area of Town: Central.
Map Reference: E 7.
Phone Number: 602-326-9686.
Directions: Located at 2150 N. Alvernon Way this is very easy to find; just
    south of Grant Rd. on Alvernon Way on the east side of the street.
Best Time of Year: All year.
Best Time of Day: Whenever they are open.
Hours: Garden: 8:30 am to 4:30 pm, seven days.
    Gift Shop: 9:00 am to 4:00 pm Monday thru Saturday, noon thru 4:00
    pm Sundays
Rules: No Pets.

 *Flora & Fauna*

Fees: Adults $3.00; Seniors (over 62) $2.00; children under 12 free.
Facilities: Restrooms, picnic area, gift shop, wheelchair accessible
Nearby Places of Interest: Reid Park Zoo.

Comments:

Tucson Botanical Gardens provides a wonderful oasis of quiet with an opportunity for a break from the hustle and bustle of the city, without the necessity of a 30 or 40 minute drive. Even if you aren't particularly interested in the educational aspects of the park, stop by if you need a relaxing break.

This is a very ambitious facility with everything from a tropical plant greenhouse to a xeriscape demonstration garden showing how low-water-use plants can be used to create a colorful landscape year round. A fine cactus garden contains local species and others from around the world. There are flowers to be seen everywhere, some familiar and many exotic.

An interesting experience is to duck into the Tohono O'odham ceremonial round house and realize how much cooler it is on a hot day without benefit of any modern cooling technology.

𝕋𝕌𝕉𝕋𝕌 TANQUE VERDE GREENHOUSES

Area of Town: East.
Map Reference: D 10.
Phone Number: 602-749-4414.
Directions: From midtown take Speedway or Broadway east to Wilmot and turn left on Wilmot Rd. which turns east and continues as Tanque Verde Rd. The greenhouse is way east past Houghton Rd. at 10810 East Tanque Verde Rd.
Best Time of Year: All year.
Best Time of Day: Anytime they are open.
Hours: 9:00 am to 5:00 pm, Monday through Saturday.
Rules: No smoking.
Fees: None.
Facilities: Restrooms.
Nearby Places of Interest: Saguaro National Monument (East); Tanque Verde Falls.

Comments:

This is a private nursery which grows desert plants for sale. It is included here because it has the most exotic collection of cacti in Tucson. They are mostly displayed indoors where it is cool. The light is natural and subdued, very good for taking photos, although you may need some fill flash on dull days.

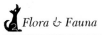

WILDFLOWERS

The fact that there are wildflowers in the desert comes as no surprise to anyone who has seen the old Walt Disney feature where the desert "blooms" with a touch of summer rain. But the reality of actually seeing a carpet of purple or golden flowers covering the arid ground as far as the eye can see is truly a wonder.

Mother nature can be fickle and some years the show is muted for a variety of reasons. The flowering bushes like the brittlebush are dependable, but the poppies, lupine and other small wildflowers responsible for the beautiful desert carpets of color are elusive.

Among the folks who care about the wildflower season in Tucson it has become a major topic of conversation every fall and spring. The fall is important because the rains must come at just the right time in December—or maybe it's October—or November. Competing theories are published in the local paper almost weekly in the fall and winter about whether the rains are coming at the right times or are the right kind or amount. In the spring there are similar articles except they are usually postmortems about why the season was or was not a stellar one.

Even in seasons where the flowers don't produce the solid carpets of color there are beautiful flowers of just about every hue growing somewhere in southern Arizona. The red **penstemon** and orange **desert-mallow** line many trails in the Tucson area. Little surprises like the **Ajo lily** and the **Arizona poppy** appear in seemingly unlikely places. Higher up in the mountains brilliant **Indian paintbrush** join the show.

Seeing the wildflowers is not like viewing historical sites. It is more like hunting, you go out and look; maybe you'll see what you came to see and maybe you won't, it depends on your luck. Nonetheless, you'll be sure to see some fine country and almost certainly some flowers.

Besides the Kitt Peak drive detailed in this section, there are a number of other popular wildflower drives from Tucson. **Picacho Peak State Park** about 45 miles north of town on I-10, sometimes produces showstopping displays of poppies. Other folks prefer the drive out North Oracle Road (Hwy 89). At Oracle Junction you can either head to Florence on the Pinal Pioneer Parkway (Hwy 89) or to Globe on Hwy 77. Either way there is plenty of opportunity to stop and enjoy fine desert vistas.

Facing Page: Brittlebush in bloom along Catalina Highway, ©PeterNoebels

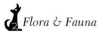

TUCSON TO KITT PEAK DRIVE

Area of Town: West.

Map Reference: W 3-4.

Phone Number: None

Directions: Take I-10 south to I-19 and get off at Ajo Way (Hwy. 86), turn right (west) and keep going. It's about 40 miles to the Kitt Peak turn. If you decide to visit Kitt Peak on this trip it's just a few miles off the highway. See page 157 for discussion of Kitt Peak.

Best Time of Year: To see the flowers, the best months are late March to early June depending entirely on the year. Ask around.

Best Time of Day: Full sun for the flowers.

Hours: All day.

Rules: Make sure you get off the roadway when you stop; no hiking without a permit on the Tohono O'Odham reservation.

Fees: None.

Facilities: Last chance for a restroom is at Three Points but you may prefer the one at the restaurant at Ryan Airfield.

Nearby Places of Interest: Kitt Peak.

Comments:

Once past the urban sprawl of Tucson, this is a very nice drive. While this trip is described as stopping at the Kitt Peak turnoff, there are very good wildflower places for a few miles past the turnoff as well. The main attraction (when they show up) are the golden **poppies**. In places there are also thick carpets of purple **lupine** or **owl clover**.

Bright red blooms on the stalks of the **ocotillo** are likely in a good year. They will often be seen together with enormous masses of bright yellow

flowers on the **giant prickly pear** plants to be seen along the roadside, especially just past the Kitt Peak turnoff. A little later, in May and June the **saguaros** will put out their beautiful white blossoms.

Facing Page: Owl clover and five-needle marigold near Kitt Peak,
© Randy Prentice

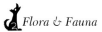

ASPEN LOOP TRAIL

Area of Town: Northeast, Santa Catalina Mountains.

Map Reference: See map on page 43.

Phone Number: 602-749-8700 (Santa Catalina Ranger District).

Directions: Take Grant Rd. or Speedway Blvd. to Tanque Verde Rd. to the Catalina Highway sign then go left and follow the road for 30 miles as it winds up the mountain. Fill up with gas before you go, <u>there is no gas at the top of Mount Lemmon</u>. Drive all the way up the mountain (about an hour) and through the village of Summerhaven to Marshall Gulch and park. The trailhead is marked in the parking lot.

Best Time of Year: When the leaves change colors varies from year to year but a good bet is the second or third week in October.

Best Time of Day: It will be cold in the early morning so you probably want to wait until the sun has been up for a while.

Hours: 24 hours.

Rules: Pets on leash; take all your trash back down with you; do not drink and drive anywhere but especially not on the Mount Lemmon Highway.

Fees: None.

Facilities: Several good picnic areas along the road with restrooms and drinking water. Camping available at Rose Canyon Lake, General Hitchcock and Molino Basin. Lodgings are available in several small lodge/bed & breakfast places in Summerhaven, the village at the top. Also, there are a couple of good places to eat in Summerhaven. The chili at the Iron Door Restaurant at the Ski Valley is a local favorite.

Nearby Places of Interest: There is a description of attractions on the Catalina Highway on page 41.

Around Summerhaven there are places to stroll on the roads to see the fall colors without much of a hike with the bonus of seeing maple trees flaming with fall crimson contrasting with the golden aspen.

Another possibility is to take the ski lift to Radio Ridge and then head right (east) to the **Aspen Draw Trail** and take it downhill for 1.6 miles to the ski lodge. An alternative at the top of the ski lift is to head left (west) to the **Sabino Dawn Trail** and take it downhill 1.2 miles through a fir forest to the ski lodge. The colors will be better on the Aspen Draw Trail.

Comments:

The Aspen Loop hike passes through glades of aspens mixed with ponderosa pine. When the aspen turn golden in the fall the light seems to make the air glow. Even when they are past their peak for color, the white straight trunks against the blue sky are striking.

The hike is not too arduous, although it does go uphill at first. Plan on about two hours to cover the 3.7 miles plus time for stops to rest and enjoy the views. There are several places about 3/4 of the way around where short side trails lead off to good lookout points where you can see the valley and the **Summit Crags**.

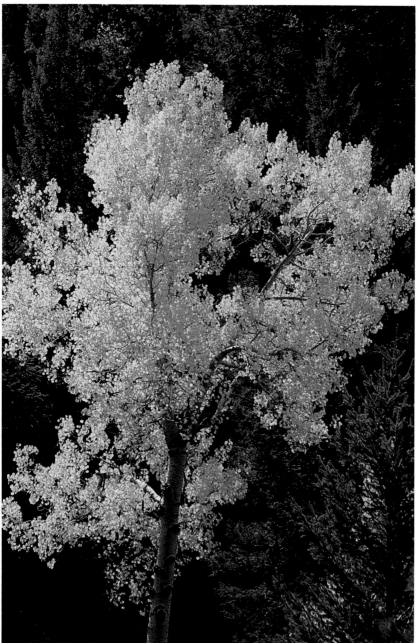

Aspen in fall garb on Mt. Lemmon, © Edward McCain

There are fine opportunities to see wildlife around Tucson. A drive on any road in **Saguaro National Monument** (East or West)) will be sure to provide sightings of cactus wrens, quail, rabbits, different species of, **hawks**, **lizards** of a bewildering variety and many other possibilities. **Deer** and **coyote** are often seen around sunset, as are **javelina**, the bristly wild pigs resembling miniature wild boars.

But for the easiest access to good viewing and to see the exotic animals like mountain lions and Mexican wolves, a trip to the **Arizona-Sonora Desert Museum** is a must. There you will enjoy unfettered views of animals in natural settings. From the famous hummingbird enclosure to the artificial mountain built for the desert bighorn sheep you will encounter settings designed to make the animals at home.

Reid Park Zoo has very good facilities for its tenants. The open enclosures also allow clear views of tigers, elephants and the like in natural settings.

For those who would like a close encounter with big game animals from around the world, and don't mind that they aren't alive, there is the **International Wildlife Museum**. Housed in a castle-like structure, this facility has collections of mounted big game animals. Included are lions, water buffalo and rhinos, polar bears, musk oxen and a lot more. These animals are very easy to photograph as they don't move around much.

Photo Tips: When using flash on animals that are behind glass, like the rattlesnakes at the Desert Museum, you can avoid the reflection of the flash in the glass if you use a PC or off-camera cord to remotely connect the flash to the camera. Hold the flash separate from the camera and at a 45 degree angle to the glass. If your flash is built-in you won't be able to do this.

You will want a long lens to shoot the animals in the enclosures. Remember you must use a tripod to avoid fuzzy pictures if you use a shutter speed lower than the focal length of your lens. For, example if you are shooting with your zoom at 210mm you will have to use a shutter speed of at least 1/250 sec to get a clear shot when hand holding the camera. A powerful flash can help with this problem, especially the newer ones that take the calculation out of using flash with zoom lenses. Small built-in flashes will only work to about 15 feet or so, depending on the speed of the film you are using.

Facing Page: Little big horns learning to climb, © Edward McCain

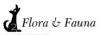

ARIZONA-SONORA DESERT MUSEUM

Area of Town: West.

Map Reference: E 2; see also map on page 54-55.

Phone Number: 602-883-1380.

Directions: Take Speedway west past I-10. As it winds up into the Tucson Mountains it changes names to Gates Pass Rd. Follow this through the pass and down the other side where the road intersects with Kinney Rd. at a stop sign. Go right and within two miles you will see the museum on the left. If you are towing a trailer or don't like mountain passes, go south on I-10 and exit on Ajo Rd. Go west (right) and continue on Ajo Way to Kinney Rd. on the other side of the Tucson Mountains. At the light, make a right and follow Kinney Rd. to the Desert Museum.

Best Time of Year: All year but in summer it will be hot after 9:00 am.

Best Time of Day: The early morning and late afternoon light are best for viewing and photographs. Also, the animals may be more active at those times. In the winter, when it is cool, mid-day may be just fine.

Hours: October through February: 8:30 am to 5:00 pm.
March through September: 7:30 am to 6:00 pm.

Rules: No pets; no picnicking on museum grounds.

Fees: Adults $7.95; Children 6 to 12 years old $1.50; children under 6 years old are free.

Facilities: Restaurant; gift shop; restrooms; wheelchair access. Camping and picnicking are not available at the museum but are available nearby in Tucson Mountain Park.

Nearby Places of Interest: Saguaro National Monument (West); Old Tucson; Gates Pass.

Comments:

The **mountains lions** are perennial favorites at the Desert Museum. It is thrilling to hear them scream late in the afternoon as they pace in and out of their caverns and through the vegetation making up their enclosure. A photograph of a lion in this setting with the hint of motion caused by their pacing can be surprisingly realistic.

On the other end of the scale are the **river otters** who looks like they would love to play Frisbee with the visitors if they could. They cruise around the little pond in the shade and stare up with warm brown eyes.

The **chuckwallas** are ferocious looking lizards which provide endless entertainment as they scamper around their rock home glaring at the visitors.

The javelina family liesaround blissfully all day with tiny babies often the center of their concern. There is a surprising amount of smooching among the adults, proving that beauty is in the eye of the beholder.

Late in the day the visitor pressure lets up some, especially in the warmer weather. Even when it has been 100 degrees in the full heat of the afternoon, the last hour or so of the day can be pleasant. If you are around when it rains you will see even more activity among the residents.

Prairie dog

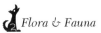

REID PARK ZOO

Area of Town: Midtown.

Map Reference: E 7.

Directions: The entrance is on 22nd St. between Country Club Rd. and Alvernon Way on the north side of the street.

Best Time of Year: All year.

Hours: Monday-Friday 8:30 am to 3:30 pm. Saturday and Sunday 8:30 am to 5:30 pm.

Rules: No pets.

Fees: Age 0-5, free; 5-14, 75 cents; 15-61, $3.00; seniors, $2.00.

Facilities: Restrooms, giftshop, snackbar.

Nearby Places of Interest: El Presidio Neighborhood; Tucson Botanical Gardens.

Comments:

This is a fine small zoo with a number of first-rate animal enclosures constructed in recent years. The fabulous Siberian tigers can usually be seen in their jungle-like setting and are startling even at rest. Oddly enough, even in the intense heat of summer there is considerable mid-day activity among many of the animals like the **African antelope**, **giraffes**, and **elephants**. The waterfowl can be positively hectic, even in temperatures around 100 degrees. The Malayan **sun bear** appears oblivious to people and sometimes lounges near the glass view window into his outdoor enclosure.

Reid Park Zoo definitely rates a visit.

Rhino feeding, Reid Park Zoo

Flora & Fauna

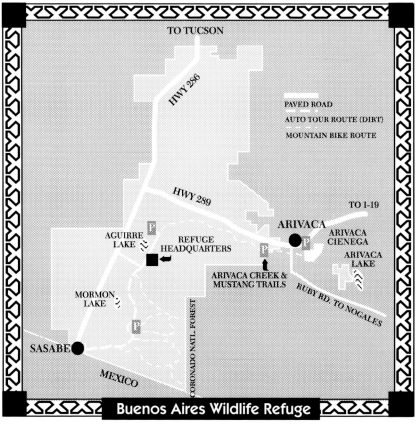

Buenos Aires Wildlife Refuge

🔲🔲🔲 BUENOS AIRES WILDLIFE REFUGE

Area of Town: 40 miles southwest.

Map Reference: Y 3; see also map of Arivaca on page 160.

Phone Number: 602-823-4251.

Directions: Take I-10 to I-19 and go south and exit on Ajo Way Head west on Ajo (Hwy 86) for about 25 miles to Three Points (Robles Junction), then take Hwy 286 south for about 30 miles to the refuge headquarters.

Best Time of Year: After the rains the tanks will fill and there will be the maximum bird life, but there are critters to see all year if you are patient. Ranging from 3,200 feet to 4,600 feet in elevation the Refuge is a little cooler than Tucson.

Best Time of Day: Early and late for the light and to see wildlife.

Hours: 24 hours; refuge headquarters 7:30 am to 4:00 pm M-F.

Rules: Pets on leash; no off road driving.

Fees: None

Facilities: A Visitor Center is being developed; restrooms; camping is permitted at designated locations but there are no facilities.

95

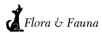

Nearby Places of Interest: Sasabe, a tiny border town is seven miles south on Hwy 286; 12 miles to the east on Hwy 289 (paved with gravel) is the village of Arivaca; Rancho de la Osa serves an elegant lunch in a historic setting.

Comments:

This trip is for nature lovers. Although there are excellent views of Kitt Peak and Baboquivari Peak from the highway, there are not the kind of dramatic views available, for example, along the Mount Lemmon Highway. But there are fine wildflowers including soaptree yuccas, the big white bell flowers of the datura (loco weed) and the great desert poppy and many, many others.

The 115,000 acre ranch was acquired by the United States Fish and Wildlife Service to be managed for the reintroduction of **masked bobwhite quail** which were wiped out it the late 1800's as a result of cattle ranching. Overgrazing changed an area described by early explorers as "a rolling sea of grass" into the typical cattle country you see today with lots of "range invader" mesquite trees. Later a population of antelope, native but hunted out, was reintroduced. Despite severe predation of the newborn by coyotes, the antelopes now seem to be holding their own.

What makes this area special are the numerous seasonal ponds which draw bird life, especially in the summer when the tanks fill from the thunderstorms. There is also permanent water in the stream and wetlands near **Arivaca**.

There are several trails to hike, and mountain biking roads are also designated. Mountain bikes must stay on the roads. **Antelope Drive,** starting near the headquarters and coming out in Sasabe, is a nice dirt road where you can look for birds, antelope and deer; take binoculars.

At one time wolves, black bears and jaguar roamed this area, but they have been gone since the beginning of intensive ranching in the late 1800's. Still, a jaguar was treed by a rancher's dogs near Baboquivari Peak in 1992. Today you will commonly see mule deer, white tail deer, antelope, coyotes and javelina. Also common in the area but less often seen are mountain lions, badgers, coatimundi and ring-tailed cats.

INTERNATIONAL WILDLIFE MUSEUM

Area of Town: West.
Map Reference: E 5.
Phone Number: 602-624-4024.
Directions: Go west on Speedway, five miles past I-10 and about half way up into the Tucson Mountains you will see a large castle structure on the right. This is it!

Best Time of Year: All year.

Hours: 9:00 am to 5:00 pm, open holidays except Christmas, New Years and Thanksgiving.

Rules: No smoking.

Fees: $5.00 adults; $3.75 senior citizens, military & students; $1.50 children (6-12 years); children 5 and under free.

Facilities: Restrooms; restaurant, film theater, gift shop.

Nearby Places of Interest: Gates Pass; Old Tucson.

Comments:

If you have a bad attitude about hunting this is not the place for you. Hundreds of glorious animals grin their last grin at you from poses chosen by the taxidermist. But it is undeniable that their grandeur is preserved and this is a world-class collection—finer than any public natural history museum. There are good interpretive materials and films are offered. Finally, there is the chance to snack on a buffalo burger in the nice restaurant.

This place is well air-conditioned, a big plus if you are fried from the heat. Flash photography is permitted so you can still get your pictures.

Arizona has been occupied by Native Americans since at least 11,000 BC. **Hohokam** Indians farmed the Tucson area from 100 AD, when the Santa Cruz River flowed above ground year round. A pit house dated at about 700 to 900 AD has been excavated beneath downtown Tucson.

One explanation of the name Tucson comes from the Indian name Chukson. The word "chuk" means dark mountain and "son" means "foot of." **Pima Indians** had a settlement at the foot of "A" Mountain (composed of dark, volcanic rock) near modern downtown Tucson when the Spanish arrived.

Spanish explorers traveled through the Tucson area in the 1500's but it was not until the Jesuit missionary Father Eusebio Francisco Kino arrived in 1691 that colonization started here. To deal with the troublesome Indians of the northern frontier of New Spain, the Spanish devised a combination of incentives and coercion to encourage the Indians to accept the Spanish presence. The missionaries brought cattle, sheep and horses, and introduced new crops as well as the Holy Catholic Church. They also helped the more peaceful Indians defend themselves (and the Spanish) from more hostile tribes. By the time **Father Kino** returned to visit in 1699 the process was well under way. The following is an excerpt from his diary describing a visit to **Mission San Xavier del Bac** on October 29, 1699:

> *On the 29th, at about two in the afternoon and after traveling 10 leagues [about 25 miles], we arrived at San Xavier del Bac in the land of the western Sobaipuris. More than 40 children, all with crosses in their hands, came out to receive us. The road was cleaned and lined with crosses and arches. Then, bearing foods of many kinds, more than 300 hundred adults arrived. Later we counted over a thousand souls for soon others came from farther away. In anticipation of the arrival of a (resident) Father there was an earthen-roofed adobe house, and they had cattle and sheep, more than 30 head of each, a harvest of maize, a good planting of wheat—which was already sprouting—and the 66 remounts (for the expedition). We butchered two fat steers and a sheep. Pastures and planting fields are so extensive, with so many earthen aqueducts filled with plentiful water, that Father Visitor [Kino's Jesuit superior] remarked that an outlay such as theirs in this glorious valley could provision another city as large as Mexico City.*

It should be remembered that Father Kino was motivated to paint a rosy picture of the prospects because the Viceroy in Mexico City was not inclined to spend money on the northern frontier. It had not yielded easy riches like the conquest of the Aztecs. Nonetheless, there is ample evidence that numerous Indians welcomed the missionaries, although many later regretted it.

Despite the missionary activity it was not until **1775** that **Presidio San Augustin del Tucson** was founded. This was a fortification built to protect the missionaries, friendly Indians and other settlers from the hostile Indians, especially the **Apaches**.

Tucson became a Mexican city in **1821** when Mexico gained its independence from Spain. In **1854**, shortly after the **Mexican-American War of 1848**, the United States made Mexico an offer it couldn't refuse and purchased a huge area of southern Arizona, including Tucson, as part of the **Gadsden Purchase**.

In the 1850's Tucson was part of the rough and ready American West with Apaches, ranchers, dragoons and miners fighting it out for land, gold and survival. In 1862 the **Confederate** flag was raised over Tucson. This indirectly hastened the end of the Apaches. Up to then the Apaches only had to deal with small U.S. Army detachments from the east who often were not great horsemen. But with the outbreak of the Civil War, the government in Washington determined to secure Arizona and sent 3,000 California soldiers known as the **California Column,** to occupy the territory. Many of these soldiers were good horsemen and were experienced with desert terrain. The Apaches attempted to ambush a part of the column at **Apache Pass** southeast of Tucson but were routed in their first encounter with modern artillery. They were on the run for the next twenty-five years and were finally confined to reservations.

For many years in the twentieth century Tucson grew apace as folks from the world over sought the climate and space of southern Arizona. The University drew students who became permanent residents as they adopted the desert as home. Many came seeking the dry air for their health.

During **World War II** southern Arizona became a major training area for aviators. **Davis-Monthan** and other air bases appeared on the desert and thousands got their first look at the southwest. Many liked what they saw and returned after the war. Air-conditioning developed during the 1950's helped decide the issue of growth and Tucson burgeoned into a metropolis of 700,000 people by 1993.

NATIVE AMERICAN CULTURE

The earliest Native Americans in the Tucson area did not leave much in the way of architecture. There are many pit house sites which have been excavated but nothing on the scale of Casa Grande, 50 miles north. A great deal of pottery and artifacts have been gathered and give some hints at the culture that produced them. Also, the oral traditions of the Tohono O'Odham people are a rich source of knowledge about these pre-columbian people. The **Arizona State Museum** just inside the University Main Gate and the nearby **Arizona Historical Society Heritage Center** both have interesting collections and interpretive material. The **Amerind Foundation** near Dragoon has an impressive collection of Indian pottery and artifacts.

For sightseeing though, the most fascinating Native American legacy are the haunting **petroglyphs** and **pictographs** left by these people. There are excellent examples throughout the Tucson area.

There is living heritage of the old Native American ways as well. For example, the **Yaqui Indians** have an elaborate annual festival at the **Pascua Yaqui Village**, in southwest Tucson. The event held several nights during Easter week melds Catholic religion and tribal rites in the Yaquis' unique interpretation of the crucifixion of Jesus Christ.

The strong influence of the Native American spiritual beliefs on the Catholic Church is nowhere more obvious than at **Mission San Xavier del Bac**. The collection of statuary and decoration depict the usual religious figures, but sometimes with a demonic twist reflecting tribal beliefs predating the coming of the Spanish.

Facing Page: Petroglyphs on Signal Hill, Saguaro National Monument (West),
© Randy Prentice

SIGNAL HILL PETROGLYPHS

Area of Town: West.

Map Reference: D 2; see also map on page 12.

Phone Number: 602-883-6366 (Monument Headquarters)

Directions: There are detailed directions on getting to the west unit of Saguaro National Monument on page 11. **Signal Hill Picnic Area** is located just off Golden Gate Road about a mile and a half east of Sandario Rd. There is a path to the little hill where the petroglyphs are located just north of the picnic area .

Best Time of Year: All year.

Best Time of Day: Early and late for the good light, midday in winter if it is cool.

Hours: 24 hours.

Rules: Pets must be leashed and are not allowed on trails.

Fees: None.

Facilities: Restrooms and drinking water. Visitor Center has ranger on duty and sells maps and books. Picnicking but no camping.

Nearby Places of Interest: King Canyon petroglyphs; Arizona-Sonora Desert Museum; Old Tucson; Gates Pass.

Comments:

This area has been inhabited for at least eight thousand years and ancient trails, shrines and sleeping circles have been identified. The petroglyphs were probably made by **Hohokam Indians** who lived in the **Tucson Mountains** from 700 to 1300 AD. Scholars are unsure whether the petroglyphs are artistic expressions or communications of some sort. Regardless, they are striking, especially with the expansive background spread out behind them.

KING CANYON PETROGLYPHS

Area of Town: West.

Map Reference: E 2; see also map on page 12.

Phone Number: 602-883-6366 (Saguaro National Monument (West).

Directions: Follow the directions on page 92 for the Arizona-Sonora Desert Museum. Just across Kinney Rd. from the Desert Museum is a small unmarked parking lot. From here there is a jeep road heading up the hill. There is also a signed path just to the left; this leads directly into the canyon. I would suggest you do this hike as a loop and take the jeep road in to get overall views of the canyon and the area, and then hike back down the canyon to your car. Where you see the **Mam-a-gah picnic area** the trail drops into the canyon. You have hiked 0.9 mile. Go down the canyon (really just a wash here) a few hundred yards or so. Below a small, filled-in dam you will encounter the petroglyphs.

Best Time of Year: All year but only very early in the day from June to October, unless the thunderstorms have cooled things off a lot.

Best Time of Day: The best lighting will be early and late but it may be cold in the winter until the sun warms up the canyon.

Hours: 24 hours.

Rules: No pets on trail; no alcohol.

Fees: None.

Facilities: There is a restroom at the Mam-a-gah picnic area.

Nearby Places of Interest: Signal Hill petroglyphs; Arizona-Sonora Desert Museum; Old Tucson; Gates Pass.

Comments:

This is an easy hike and should take about 20 or 30 minutes each way. Take some water anyway; there is none at the picnic area. There is often water in the creek but it needs to be treated.

Even though the water in the creek may not be potable, it does support a variety of flowers. The **little waterfalls** are also pretty when there is a lot of water in the creek. The petroglyphs are extensive and were probably made by the same Hohokam Indian people as those at Signal Hill.

If you hike out the wash you will encounter a shelf of bedrock extending into the creek just before the road. There is an excellent conical **metate** in it. A metate is a hole in which Indians placed mesquite beans to be ground for food. The grinding was done with another rock used as a pestle.

When you get back down the canyon to the road you may spot the path that leads back up to the parking lot. If you don't, just make a left at the road to return.

MISSION SAN XAVIER DEL BAC

Area of Town: Southwest.
Map Reference: F 5.
Phone Number: 602-294-2624.
Directions: Take I-10 to I-19 and go south several miles and exit at San Xavier Rd. The mission is about 1/2 mile west.
Best Time of Year: All year.
Best Time of Day: Early and late for the best light.
Hours: You can visit the site to take pictures anytime but the building and gift shop is only open from 8:00 am to 6:00 pm. This is an active church. Masses are held daily at 8:30 am. Sunday services are at 8:00, 9:30, 11:00 am and at 12:30 pm.
Rules: No flash photography during services.
Fees: Donations are appropriate to help with the ongoing restoration.
Facilities: Gift shop, restrooms, food and native American handicraft vendors in season.
Nearby Places of Interest: El Presidio Neighborhood; Barrio Historico.

Comments:

W hen the Spanish missionaries arrived in southern Arizona their objective was to bring the heathen souls of the Indians into the mother church. They also did a little mining, but mainly they were intent on building their missions (with the considerable labor of the Indians). In order to convert the Indians they fed them and introduced them to European ways.

Most importantly the Spanish soldiers helped the Indians gathered at the missions to protect themselves from predation by the other Indians. The **Pima**, **Sobaipuri**, **Maricopa** and **Yuma** tribes feuded and raided each other endlessly and violently. The **Apaches** preyed on all of them and on the Spanish.

The Indian settlement which predated the mission here was called **Bac** meaning "the places where the water appears." The Santa Cruz River flowed underground for a distance from the south but reappeared at a spot near the present site of the mission. There was extensive agriculture in many Indian settlements along the water courses in southern Arizona for centuries before the Spanish came.

In 1700 Father Eusebio Francisco **Kino** first established a church about two miles north of the present location of the mission. The current

Facing Page Top: Native American Dancers, San Xavier Fiesta & Pageant
Bottom: Mexican American Dancers, San Xavier Fiesta & Pageant,
© *Balfour Walker Photography*

building was started in 1783 and "finished" in 1797. One tower remains incomplete to this day.

This is probably the most photogenic thing—animal, vegetable or mineral—in Arizona. The white, graceful walls catch the light wonderfully and the mission forms a marvelous foreground for pictures of the enormous summer thunderheads.

The little hill just east makes a great place to watch the sunset or the sunrise any time of year.

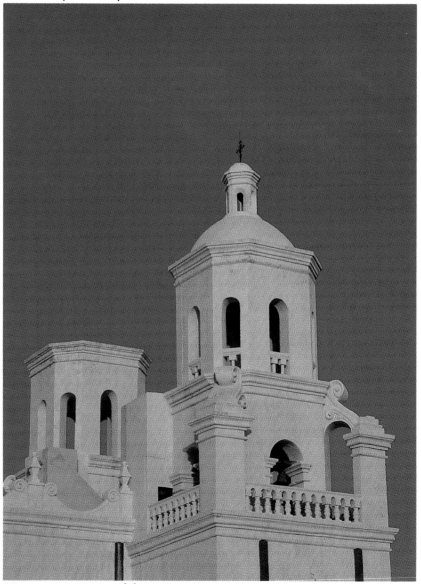

Mission San Xavier del Bac

ꡀꡀꡀꡀꡀꡀꡀꡀꡀ HISPANIC CULTURE

The first European visitors to the Tucson area were Spaniards who passed through over 450 years ago. Since at least the late 1600's, when Father Kino established the first church at Mission San Xavier del Bac, there has been a regular Hispanic presence.

Many of the early miners and ranchers of southern Arizona were Mexican. The **Presidio San Augustin del Tucson**, completed in **1783,** was manned at first by Spanish and later Mexican soldiers. For the next hundred years Tucson was essentially a Mexican town. In 1860, several years after Tucson officially came under American sovereignty, Hispanics still represented 71% of the population. A unique culture evolved, shaped by Spanish heritage, the desert, and the frontier isolation. Immigrants from the United States came in force only after the **Mexican-American War of 1848**. When they did, there was often intermarriage and the new Arizonans adopted much of the Hispanic way of life and attitudes.

Today you are still very likely to hear Spanish being spoken at many public places in Tucson. Tucson is a hub for a great deal of trade with **Mexico** and sees many American and Mexican tourists traveling to and from Mexico.

There are many showcases for Hispanic culture in Tucson, besides the passing parade of human life. **Mission San Xavier del Bac** discussed in the previous section is one of the finest examples of Spanish missionary architecture in the New World. The **Arizona Heritage Museum** has interesting exhibits about the settlement of the Tucson area which necessarily focus on the Hispanic influence of the early settlers from Mexico.

For living heritage, there is nothing that is more fun than the **Tucson International Mariachi Conference**. This is a fiesta of musicians, most of whom travel here from all over Mexico. The people are wonderful, the costumes are gorgeous, the music stirring and the food authentic. Don't miss it.

Speaking of food, the **Mexican restaurants** along South 4th Ave. in the city of **South Tucson** provide an excellent taste of Hispanic culture. There is a good listing of restaurants in the Tucson Official Visitors Guide available at the Visitors Center 130 S. Scott in downtown Tucson.

There are several old neighborhoods reflecting Tucson's Hispanic origins. The architecture of northern Mexico was adopted here as a practical way to deal with the desert heat. Interior courtyards allowed privacy and outdoor living. The **Barrio Historico** features good examples of this adaptive architecture. In El Presidio neighborhood **La Casa**

Cordova is a restored example that is open to the public. A fine example of upper class living is the restored **Sosa-Carrillo-Fremont House** adjacent to the Barrio Historico.

A reflection of the deep spiritual component of Hispanic culture is the enduring nature of the many informal shrines throughout southern Arizona. Not established by any formal church, nor maintained by any government or foundation, they survive on private care. One such folk shrine which has passed into the public domain is **El Tiradito** or **The Wishing Shrine**.

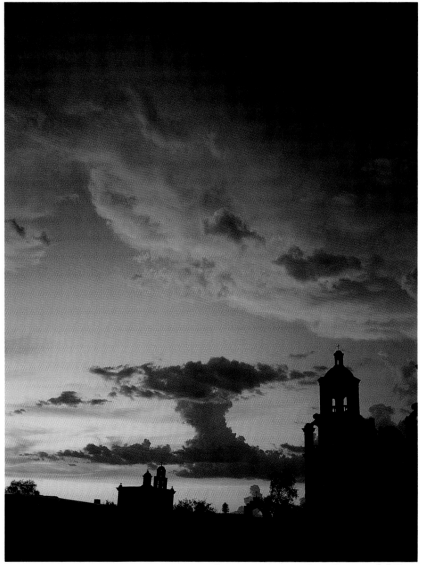

Sunset, Mission San Xavier del Bac .

𝕸𝕴𝕾𝕾 MISSION SAN XAVIER DEL BAC

The general information about the mission is set out in the previous section on Native American culture. This landmark is mentioned in both sections because it is inextricably tied to the cultural heritage of both groups in the Tucson area.

Mission San Xavier del Bac was part of an extensive chain of missions established and operated over several hundred years throughout what is now Mexico and the American Southwest. The chain was connected by mule trains that covered thousands of miles and took months to reach their destinations. Another example covered in this guide is **Mission San Jose de Tumacacori**.

By the time construction was started on the mission in **1783**, the Spanish already had been in Mexico for over 270 years. That is longer than the current United States has existed, including most of its colonial origins. During those centuries the Spanish and their culture melded with the indigenous people and their culture to form a new and vital Mexican or Hispanic culture.

The demonic appearance of some of the statues in the mission are evidence of cultural influences both Mexican and purely Native American. But the main themes of the Roman Catholic religion depicted throughout the mission make plain that the purpose of the missionaries was to bring souls into a clearly traditional Roman Catholic church.

Examine the details in this structure: the rattlesnake handle on the front door and the cat and the mouse on opposite sides above, the cat apparently chasing the mouse. The little bell tower above the mortuary chapel on the west side of the church makes a nice silhouette to see or photograph the sunset through.

BARRIO HISTORICO

Area of Town: Downtown.

Map Reference: E 6.

Phone Number: 602-624-1817 (Tucson Visitors Bureau).

Directions: Look at the map on the inside front cover and take the most direct route downtown from wherever you are. Park near the south side of the Community Center and use the detail map on the next page for directions.

Best Time of Year: All year.

Best Time of Day: Early and late for the best light.

Hours: For the light see the sunrise/sunset table in Appendix Two.

Rules: People live in these houses so show common courtesy for their privacy.

Fees: None.

Facilities: There are restrooms in the Community Center and there are several restaurants in the area. El Minuto at the corner of Cushing St. and Main is famous for the Mexican hangover remedy it is named after. The Cushing Street Bar at Cushing St. and Convent has good food and drinks in a territorial setting.

Nearby Places of Interest: El Presidio; Old Court House at Pennington and Church; Tucson City Library across from the Old Court House.

Comments:

When the priests, soldiers, artisans, ranchers and their families came north the thousands of miles from Mexico to build and populate the Presidio at Tucson, they brought their Mexican culture with them. The architecture had to adapt itself to the desert environment, but also was molded by the extended family structure which was (and is today) a central feature of Mexican culture.

The surviving Barrio Historico is not extensive but it is sufficient to give a flavor of the old days. The walls of the houses were built almost to the street, with the open space reserved for the courtyard inside which was part of the living area used by the large families.

The materials used were adobe brick made of local mud and straw. The soft adobe walls were built two feet or more thick to provide strength for support. A most beneficial result is that these adobe homes are cool even in the summer heat. In order to protect the soft adobe from disintegrating in the rain the walls are plastered.

The plastered walls with graceful curves and deep-set windows and doors make eye-pleasing pictures. Many of the buildings have been restored to one extent or another and the cheerful shutters and other touches make charming additions to the urban scene.

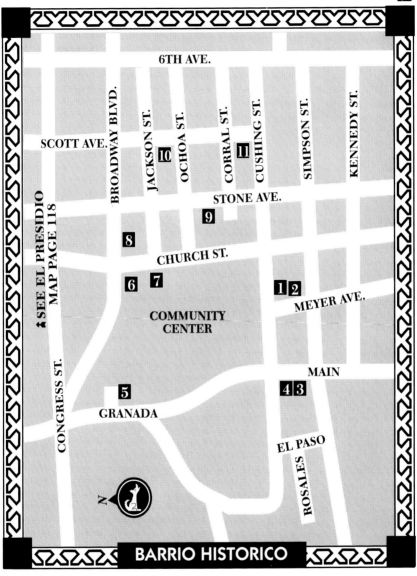

1. Cushing St. Bar & Restaurant
2. America West Gallery
3. El Tiradito
4. El Minuto Mexican Restaurant
5. Sosa Carrillo-Freemont House
6. La Placita Village
7. Samniego House
8. Old Adobe Mexican Restaurant
9. St. Augustine Cathedral
10. Tucson Visitors Center
11. Temple of Music & Art

SOSA-CARRILLO-FREMONT HOUSE
(aka Casa del Gobernador)

Area of Town: Downtown.
Map Reference: E 6.
Phone Number: 602-622-0956.
Directions: Look the Barrio Historico Map on page 111. Walk through the Community Center grounds to the Music Hall and then walk around the back to the Casa. Or, if you are going directly to the Casa, drive on Granada and turn into the parking lot behind the Music Hall or park at a meter on Calle Carlos Arruza, the little street just beyond.
Best Time of Year: All year.
Best Time of Day: Anytime.
Hours: Wednesday through Saturday, 10 am to 4 pm.
Rules: No smoking; no pets.
Fees: None; donation encouraged.
Facilities: Small bookstore; restroom.
Nearby Places of Interest: El Presido Neighborhood; Barrio Historico; "A" Mountain.

Comments:

This fine restoration represents how a well-to-do family was housed in Tucson in the 1880's. The restoration is complete with period furniture and personal effects.

The land was originally owned by a family named **Sosa**. It is not known whether they built a house on it. The **Carrillos** built the current house in 1880 but it was rented to **John Fremont**, the new governor of the territory. He and his wife may have lived there or maybe they only let their daughter live there. The Fremont family only used the house for 5 months and then the Carrillos occupied it for ninety years. This confusion has lead to the curious hyphenated name of the current facility operated by the **Arizona Historical Society**.

The setting of the house tells a lot about the fate of most of the Barrio Historico. The house cowers in the shadow of the huge concrete loading docks of the Tucson Community Center which has spread over blocks of formerly residential neighborhoods.

Still, it is a pleasant spot and has a good view of **"A" Mountain** which you should visit while you are downtown. Also, this is a great place to watch **fireworks** on the **4th of July**.

Facing Page: Barrio Historico, © Edward McCain

EL TIRADITO
(The Wishing Shrine)

Area of Town: Downtown.

Map Reference: E 6; see also map on page 111.

Phone Number: 602-624-1817 (Tucson Visitors Bureau).

Directions: Look at the map on the inside front cover and take the most direct route downtown from wherever you are. The shrine is located just left (south) of **El Minuto,** the Mexican restaurant on the corner of Cushing St. and Main. There should be a parking spot nearby on the street.

Best Time of Year: All year.

Best Time of Day: Anytime.

Hours: 24 hours, but I wouldn't be here much after dark.

Rules: This is an active shrine. While you may only be curious others may be here to pay their respects and ask help. Be sensitive to their feelings.

Fees: None.

Facilities: Restrooms across the street in the Community Center.

Other Nearby Places of Interest: El Presidio Neighborhood; "A" Mountain.

Comments:

All over southern Arizona and Mexico you will see these little shrines with the candles burning. This one has a special history.

According to legend an illicit love affair lead to the violent death of a young man on this site and he was buried here. Of the many versions of the story, the following was adopted by the Tucson City Council in 1927 when the site was donated to the city by its owner, Teofilo Otero:

A young sheepherder who lived with his wife and father-in-law on a ranch north of town became infatuated with his mother-in-law, who lived in town. One day he took an opportunity to come visit her and was surprised in his adulterous liaison when his father-in-law found him with his young wife. In an ensuing struggle the father-in-law killed the young man and fled to Mexico. The sheepherder was buried unceremoniously where he had fallen.

According to the legend, if the candle stays lit all night your prayer will be answered.

Facing Page: El Tiradito (The Wishing Shrine), © Randy Prentice

TERRITORIAL DAYS 🪶🪶🪶🪶🪶🪶🪶

Tucson became part of the United States in 1853 when southern Arizona was acquired from Mexico as part of the **Gadsden Purchase**. Initially part of **New Mexico Territory**, the **Arizona Territory** became a separate entity in 1863.

The main order of business in early Tucson was staying alive. Except for their cousins, the equally warlike **Navajos**, the **Apaches** had dominated the other tribes in Arizona. They and the Navajos had been raiding deep into Mexico every fall for over a hundred years, bringing back Mexican women, children and huge herds of sheep. In a five-year period in the 1770's Apaches killed over 1,900 people and stole 68,000 sheep in raids into Mexico.

As part of the **Treaty of Guadalupe Hidalgo** by which the **Mexican-American War** was settled in 1848, the United States agreed to control the raiding and the Mexicans agreed not to pursue the Apaches and Navajos into the United States.

The U.S. Army was sent to Arizona to keep the Apaches from raiding. The Apaches could understand why the Army did not want them raiding the Anglo settlers, but could not understand why the Americans wanted to protect their recent enemies the Mexicans. Relations broke down and the Apaches terrorized southern Arizona. Most ranches and mines were wiped out by the early 1860's.

Tucson was one of the few safe places and one did not wander far from town. After the withdrawal of the Mexican troops from Tucson in 1856, the raiding Chiricauhua Apaches were barely kept at bay with a small unit of United States Dragoons (heavily armed Cavalry) and a contingent of White Mountain Apache scouts working for the army.

Fort Lowell was established in 1872 near Tucson as part of the Army's efforts to defeat the Apaches. It became an important military post as the headquarters of the **Sixth United States Cavalry**. With the surrender of **Geronimo** in 1886, the war with the Apaches ended and the need for the fort did as well. It was abandoned in 1891.

A stop on the short-lived **Butterfield Overland Stage Route**, Tucson had a population of about 600 in 1860. With the arrival of the **California Column** in 1862, the Apaches were subdued to some extent and the mines and ranches of southern Arizona were reopened and expanded. Tucson was the commercial center and became the **Territorial Capital** in 1867. When the **Southern Pacific Railroad** was laid to Tucson in 1880 the population had grown to 7,000. In 1885 the civilizing influence of the **University of Arizona** was added.

Territorial days ended in 1912 when Arizona became a state. By then the town had telephones, streetcars and all the modern amenities of the day. But it also had a history of rough and ready cowboys, deadly Apaches and bad guys of all sorts which, even today, sets Arizona a little apart from the rest of the United States.

EL PRESIDIO NEIGHBORHOOD TOUR

Area of Town: Downtown.
Map Reference: E 6; see map next page.
Phone Number: 602-624-2333 (Tucson Museum of Art & Casa Cordova).
Directions: Look at the map on the inside front cover and drive, bike or walk downtown in the most direct way from where you are located. Referring to the map on the following page, locate the parking lot (**#1**) on the southwest corner of **Paseo Redondo** and **Main**. Then follow the tour.
Best Time of Year: All year.
Best Time of Day: Early and late for the light, business hours if you want to eat or shop.
Hours: 24 hours, but see the hours of some of the stops below.
Rules: Pets on leash; but you may have to leave your friend outside some establishments.
Fees: None, unless your charge card gets worked over in the galleries or book stores.
Facilities: Restrooms in the Old Courthouse (1st floor, north wing).
Nearby Places of Interest: Barrio Historico; Tucson City Library (Across from the Old Courthouse).

Comments:

There is a lot to see here and it relates to history, heritage and modern times. Follow the map on the next page, using the numbers keyed to the map. Walk up Paseo Redondo to Main. Just across the street is the **Stevens House (#2)** built in 1856. It is typical of other Tucson houses of the period, being built out to the street with the rear open and part of the living quarters. **Hiriam Stevens**, a businessman and politician, married **Petra Santa Cruz,** the Mexican granddaughter of his washer woman. They entertained and traveled together for years until Hiriam inexplicably shot her and himself in 1893. He died but she lived, saved by a silver comb in her hair. Today the house is occupied by **Janos**, a very fine restaurant.

Turning right down Main, you come to the **Edward Nye Fish House** (**#3**) on the corner of Alameda and Main. Mr. Fish, a successful store and flour mill owner, built the house in 1868. Today it is home to **El Presidio**

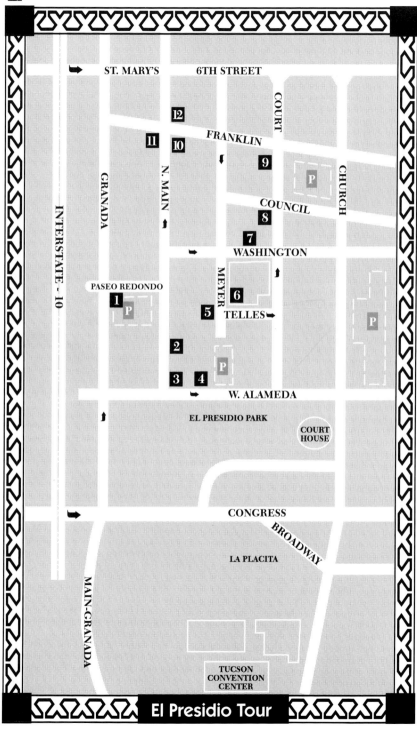

Art Gallery and you can visit the interior during business hours to appreciate the 15-foot ceilings and 2 1/2 foot thick walls. There is a lovely shaded ramada area in the rear to sit and rest.

Walk through the courtyard just to the left of the Fish house and you are in the courtyard of the **Tucson Museum of Art** (**#4**), a first-class art museum. It also has a good gift shop. A historic marker on Alameda locates the **Plaza Militar** on this spot. This was a parade ground where the soldiers exercised their horses.

Walk through the courtyard to the east and you will be in front of **La Casa Cordova** (**#5**), a restored preterritorial house reputedly started in 1848 and expanded in 1879. This is the best example of a typical adobe house from the 1800's to be seen in Tucson. The open cooking stove in the courtyard and the facilities for animals makes this representative of what it was like to actually live in a typical Tucson house in the mid 1880's. Still, it is awfully clean and, according to many contemporary travelers, Tucson of that era had a "lived-in" look. Especially amusing (accurate or not) is the account of journalist J. Ross Browne who passed through in 1864[1]. He referred to Tucson as:

> *"...the most wonderful scatteration of human habitations his eye ever beheld—a city of mud-boxes, dingy and dilapidated, cracked and baked into a composite of dust and filth; littered about with broken corrals, sheds, bakeovens, carcasses of dead animals, and broken pottery; barren of verdure, parched, naked, and grimly desolate in the glare of a southern sun. Adobe walls without whitewash, inside or out, hard-earth floors, baked and dried Mexicans, sore-backed burros, coyote dogs, and terra-cotta children...."*

Well, even allowing that this fellow was an Easterner, there must have been a little truth in what he said. So, as you are looking around the spotless courtyard of La Casa Cordova imagine a few kids running around, some laundry hanging, a few dogs lying about and probably several pigs rooting for food. But it was home and a very workable solution to living in the desert without cooling, either for the house or the food.

Across from La Casa Cordova is a large enclosed courtyard which houses **Old Town Artisans** (**#6**), a colorful collection of shops featuring southwestern crafts and art. The **Courtyard Cafe** is also located here and makes a great place to stop for lunch on their shady patio.

Exit Old Town Artisans through the Courtyard Cafe patio. This will put you on Washington St. directly across from **El Rapido** Mexican Take-out (**#7**). A Tucson institution, El Rapido features traditional Mexican food to go. In season, look out for the sign hung outside informing you that there are green corn tamales, the El Rapido specialty.

[1]Browne, Adventures in Apache County, 132-133

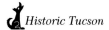

Go right on Washington and then left on Court and continue north a short way to the **Southwest Parks & Monuments Association Bookstore** (**#8**). This outstanding bookstore has an excellent collection of books, maps, guides and printed material of all sorts about the people and natural history of the Southwest. The Association is nonprofit and proceeds benefit the national parks.

Continue north on Court and you will soon pass **El Charro Cafe** and Gift Shop (**#9**). Family operated for many years, this fine Mexican restaurant also has a gift shop with some very interesting items.

Just past El Charro turn left on Franklin St. and continue to the corner of Main. There on each corner you can see the eclectic variety of architecture that evolved in Tucson from the exit of the Mexican garrison in 1856 to 1912 when Arizona became a state.

The big urban hacienda on the left now house **El Presidio Bed & Breakfast** (**#10**).

Across the street to the west is the **Steinfeld Mansion** (**#11**). This Spanish mission-style building was erected in 1900, originally as The Owls Club for a group of bachelors. It was purchased by the Steinfeld family in 1904 and served as their home.

To the right on the northeast corner of Franklin and Main is the **Rosalia Verdugo House** (**#12**). It started out in the Sonoran tradition when built in 1877 but an Anglo gabled roof was added later. To complete the confusion of identity, the original canales for draining water off the flat roof were left in place on the Main St. side.

Take a left at the corner and walk south on Main back to the car. If you still have energy walk across El Presidio Park and the Community Center grounds to the Barrio Historico or to the Sosa-Carrillo-Fremont House behind the Music Hall in the Community Center.

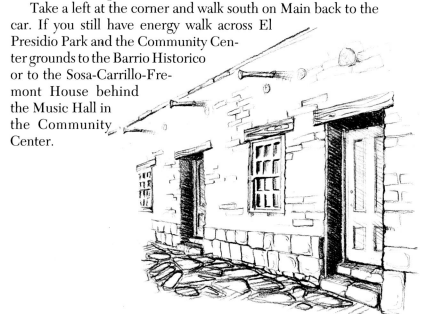

FORT LOWELL PARK & HISTORIC NEIGHBORHOOD

Area of Town: North/central.
Map Reference: D 8.
Phone Number: 602-791-2585 (Tucson Parks Dept.).
Directions: Located at Craycroft and Fort Lowell.
Best Time of Year: All year.
Best Time of Day: Early and late for the light, but the museum hours are limited, see below.
Hours: 24 hours, but the museum is only open from 10 am to 4 pm Wednesday through Saturday.
Rules: Pets on leash; no glass containers.
Fees: None.
Facilities: Restrooms; fine picnic facilities; pool.
Nearby Places of Interest: Rillito River at Craycroft; Sabino Canyon.

Comments:

When the Fort was built, a lane bordered on two sides with cotton-woods was constructed. After the Fort closed in 1891 the trees died and were chopped down. They have been replaced and with a little imagination you can imagine the off-duty soldiers strolling with the local gals who would visit the Fort for the gala band concerts and balls. Indeed, the Fort, with its contingent of dashing Cavalry officers was the social center of the rough frontier town for a period.

Now only a portion of the post hospital remains, protected from the elements by a steel ramada. Still, the small corridors and rooms almost seem to echo with the comings and goings of the busy fort. The museum is an accurate reproduction of the commanding officer's quarters. Across Craycroft a walk west along Fort Lowell Rd. will take you past several period buildings including the old officers' quarters, the commissary and the post trader's store. These are now privately occupied but the exteriors make a charming appearance and are a fine photo opportunity.

COLOSSAL CAVE

Area of Town: 15 miles southeast.

Map Reference: G 13.

Directions: East on Broadway to Old Spanish Trail (just before Camino Seco), turn right and follow Old Spanish Trail to the cave.

Best Time of Year: The temperature is 72 degrees all year in the cave.

Hours: 9:00 am to 5:00 pm.

Rules: No smoking, food or drinks in the cave.

Fees: Adults $6.50; ages 11-16, $5.00; ages 6-10, $3.50; under 5 years free.

Nearby Places of Interest: Saguaro National Monument (East).

Comments:

Colossal Cave is rich with legend and the tour guides relish laying it all out for you. Indians and outlaws used the cave and left their sign. Hidden gold and dead men are part of the heritage of the cave and you will visit the locations in the cool depths of the mountain. The extent of the cave is not in a class with Carlsbad or Kartchner Caverns but is a genuine spelunking adventure nonetheless. For most folks the 45 minute tour is plenty long.

The setting for the cave entrance is on a ridge and there are good desert views. The county park next door has a fine picnic area and good walks in the lush Sonoran Desert. The drive out from Tucson also can be recommended, offering fine views of the looming Rincon Mountains to the east.

Area of Town: Central.

Map Reference: E 6.

Phone Number: 621-2211 (University of Arizona).

Directions: See map on following page. The best parking is in the private lots one block west of the main gate.

Best Time of Year: All year.

Best Time of Day: Anytime, including the evening which can be very nice in the warm weather. If you want to walk through the building see the hours below.

Hours: You can see Old Main anytime but the building is only open from 8:30 am to 5:30 pm Monday through Friday.

Rules: No smoking.

Fees: None.

Facilities: Restrooms are available nearby in the Student Union.

Nearby Places of Interest: Arizona State Museum; Arizona Heritage Museum; Center for Creative Photography.

Comments:

There is probably no standard for what can be called territorial architecture. Nonetheless, Old Main on the University of Arizona campus fits the bill as having a peaked roof, broad porches all around and a general "airy" feel to the design.

Established in 1885 the **University of Arizona,** then known as the Arizona Territorial University, at first consisted of a single building, "Old Main," located far out on the desert from downtown Tucson. For years a street car connected the university to downtown. It has recently been reintroduced.

Besides the beautiful Old Main there is alot to see on campus and just wandering around will allow you to enjoy the beautiful grounds. Be sure to stop at the several museums in the area (see map following). For the photographer, a stop at the **Center for Creative Photography** is a must.

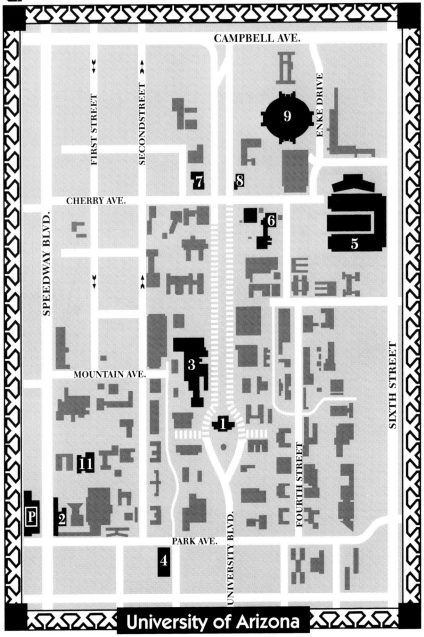

CAMPBELL AVE.

ENKE DRIVE

FIRST STREET

SECONDSTREET

CHERRY AVE.

SPEEDWAY BLVD.

SIXTH STREET

MOUNTAIN AVE.

FOURTH STREET

P

PARK AVE.

UNIVERSITY BLVD.

University of Arizona

1. Arizona Heritage Museum
2. Arizona State Museum
3. Museum of Art
4. Center for Creative Photography
5. Old Main
6. Student Union

7. Stadium & Track
8. Main Library
9. G. H. Flandrau Planetarium
10. Visitors Center
11. McKale Memorial Center
P. Park Avenue Parking Garage

𝕯𝖚𝖗𝖎𝖘𝖚𝖗𝖎𝖘𝖚𝖗𝖎𝖘𝖚𝖗𝖎 AVIATION HISTORY

Arizona's excellent weather has always made it a popular place for flying. When **World War II** demanded that pilots be trained at top speed, dozens of training fields were built all over Arizona. After the war, Davis-Monthan survived as an active base, now training pilots in tank-killing **A-10's**.

Commercial aviation also takes advantage of the great weather and **Lufthansa** and **Japan Airlines** do much of their pilot training in Arizona. **Ryan Field** west of town on Ajo Way is the center for this facility in southern Arizona. The dry desert air facilitates the storage of idle planes and there are lines of huge commercial jets stored at **Pinal Air Park** about 25 miles north of Tucson just off I-10.

Because of the dry desert climate **Davis-Monthan Air Force Base** has become the final resting place for much of the finest Air Force in the world. It is amazing to see line after line of behemoth **B-52's** with their shark fins towering above the other planes just baking in the sun. Even more amazing is to see dozens of **F-14 Tomcats**, the star of the movie **Top Gun** sitting idle.

Many planes are sold to foreign governments to recoup some of their cost. Many more are cannibalized for parts.

On a more cheerful note, the dry air has also attracted the best collection of aircraft in the world at the **Pima Air Museum**. This phenomenal facility just keeps getting better. Not to be missed.

🌀DAVIS-MONTHAN AIRCRAFT BONEYARD

Area of Town: South.
Map Reference: F 8.
Phone Number: 602-750-4570 (Base Public Affairs Office).
Directions: Drive south on Kolb Rd. to Escalante (next main road after Golf Links) and turn right (west). You will be on the northern boundary of the base and will be able to see the rows of planes through the fence. You can also see the planes as you drive south on Kolb, but you cannot stop on this busy street to look. If you are coming from I-10 or from the Pima Air Museum to the south, you will turn left off of Kolb onto Escalante. For the tour mentioned below you have to go the main gate at Craycroft and Golf Links.

Best Time of Year: Anytime.

Best Time of Day: Early and late in the day for the best light.

Hours: 24 hours; tour by reservation at 9:00 am on Monday & Wednesday only.

Rules: This is a guarded military facility so do not get ideas about getting closer to the planes than the fence.

Fees: None.

Facilities: None unless you take the tour.

Nearby Places of Interest: Pima Air Museum.

Comments:

This is truly an astounding sight, especially when you consider that many of the 4,000 planes you are looking at cost more than a good-sized high school. There is also a sadness contemplating the individualized markings the pilots and crews bestowed on their "birds," which now sit moldering in the desert. Bring your **binoculars**.

If you park at the northwest corner of Kolb and Escalante you can walk along the fence on Kolb Rd. and get a good view of the newer planes on the right. There are ranks of **F-4 Phantom** fighter-bombers that were work horses in Vietnam. Farther on you may be looking at **F-111's** that were dropping ordinance over Libya only a few short years ago. **F-14's** that were streaking through the night skies over Baghdad recently are now providing shade for prairie dogs.

Drive east from Kolb along Irvington and you will see the lines of **B-52's** in the distance. Don't worry, you can see one up close at the Pima Air Museum.

The Tour. On Monday and Wednesday you can get a free tour of the storage facility and the flight line with current air operations by calling 750-4570 and making a reservation. On the day of the tour just show up at the main gate at Craycroft and Golf Links at 8:45 am and the guard will tell you where to park. The bus will take you past the active planes on the flight line and you will get a good view of the dozens of A-10 "Tank Killers" currently based here. A good briefing from a friendly Air Force officer accompanies the driving tour, explaining why this is <u>not</u> a boneyard. You will be able to get snapshots of the base as you are driven through but quality images are hard with the bus moving most of the time. Sit on the right side of the bus to get the best pictures. Your best bet for aircraft pictures is the Pima Air Museum.

Photo Tips: Hold your camera as close as possible to the fence with the lens in the middle of the hole in the cyclone fence and chances are good you will get an acceptable image. If you are using a camera with a big zoom lens use a large aperture (f 3.5 for example) to minimize depth of field so the fence wire doesn't show. Bring a **long lens**.

Facing Page: A few of the 4,000 aircraft stored at Davis-Monthan.

Historic Tucson

PIMA AIR MUSEUM

Area of Town: South.
Map Reference: F 8.
Phone Number: 602-574-0462.
Directions: Drive south on Kolb Rd. and turn right (west) at Valencia Rd., and drive to museum entrance. If you are starting from I-10, get off at the Valencia Rd. exit and go east to the museum entrance. The address of the museum is 6000 East Valencia Rd.
Best Time of Year: All year, but avoid the middle of the day in summer.
Best Time of Day: Early and late in the day for the best light.
Hours: 9:00 am until 5:00 pm, except Christmas day; no admittance after 4:00 pm.
Rules: Pets on leash; taking photos is permitted but if it is for a commercial purpose permission must be obtained in advance.
Fees: Adults: $5.00; Military and Seniors: $4.00; Children 11 to 17 : $3.00; under 11 free.
Facilities: Restrooms; snack bar; gift shop.
Nearby Places of Interest: Davis-Monthan Aircraft Boneyard.

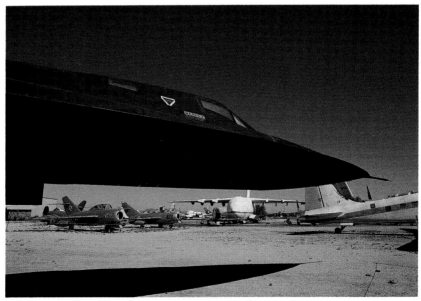

SR-71 "Blackbird" with Korean Migs in background, Pima Air Museum.

Comments:

Y ou know you are in for something special when you pull into the parking lot. Looming over the south edge of the lot is an enormous black **B-52** looking like the angel of death, as indeed it was. Big, simple (compared to today's billion-dollar bombers) and very powerful, this bomber has enforced the price of war in foreign skies for over forty years. It is still in service. Called the **"Buff"** by its pilots and crews because of its toughness and heavy buffalo-like appearance it has a firm place in aviation history.

Entering the museum you pass <u>under</u> an enormous Sikorsky "Skyhook" helicopter perching 20 feet off the ground like a metallic preying mantis. Inside, you pass through a large gift shop and into the indoor aircraft exhibit. Exhibited are the beautiful and the bizarre including the **"Busy Bee"**, the world's smallest airplane for manned flight.

The heart of the museum is the extensive outdoor collection of aircraft spreading over many acres and including the most famous aircraft of military aviation history.

Right out the back door you are confronted with the fantastic **SR-71 "Blackbird."** Recently retired after setting a speed record for coast-to-coast flight of 68 minutes this aircraft is awe-inspiring. Designed like a flying dagger its leading edges are knife-like and taper only slightly as the lines blend back to the two gargantuan jet engines. **Jetstars**, **Flying Fortresses**, **VooDoos**, **Tigercats**, **Hustlers** and **Shooting Stars** share the grounds with **Cargomasters**, **Hueys**, **Trackers**, **Beavers** and **Flying Boxcars**. There is a **Constellation** used by President Eisenhower and **Korean Mig** fighters. An **X-15** shares the indoor space exhibit with missiles produced locally at the Hughes plant.

Titan Missile Museum

Another unique bit of aviation history is operated by the museum in Green Valley about 20 miles south of Tucson on I-19. A Titan IBM missile silo, complete with missile in place, has been turned into a museum. Open to the public every day except Christmas, hours are 9:00 am to 5:00 pm, last tour at 4:00 pm. Adults $5.00, seniors/military $4.00 & juniors 10-17 $3.00. Under 10 free. Phone 602-791-2929 or 625-7736 for reservations for guided tours.

COWBOY STUFF

ounded in 1783 as a Spanish Presidio to protect missionaries and Mexican settlers from the Apaches, Tucson's development under Spanish, Mexican and American flags has included a rich and rough mixture of cowboys, miners, dragoons, Apaches, frontier women, and fast-talking entrepreneurs. They came from Spain, Mexico, the American East and around the world.

Ranching has been an important part of southern Arizona since Father Kino introduced cattle in the 1690's. Native American and Mexican cowboys, **"vaqueros,"** rode the range here for hundreds of years, and still do. Anglo cowboys from Texas and elsewhere joined them when the United States acquired southern Arizona in 1853.

Cowboys have endured in southern Arizona, not only with their distinctive dress but with an attitude toward life that they fly like a flag. You will see it here and there amid the hurly burly of modern Tucson. A young fella or a skinny old guy with blue jeans a little too long dragging the ground over worn cowboy boots. They are in from Benson or Arivaca and they are not part of the mall scene. Theirs is the "cowboy way."

The flavor of the Old West remained well into this century. Tucson stayed small and sleepy, leaping into modern tempo and rapid population growth only since World War II. Today Tucson displays its cowboy heritage best in a few notable events and places.

La Fiesta de los Vaqueros in February is without a doubt the Cowboy Event of the year in Tucson. Everybody loves Rodeo Week and all over town you will see Tucsonans dressed in their best cowperson attire. The four-day rodeo is a Professional Rodeo Cowboy Association Rodeo, and draws top contestants in all the events.

Perhaps even more appealing to sightseers and photographers alike is the **Tucson Rodeo Parade**. Billed as the longest non-mechanized parade in the world, this parade will provide you with more wild west atmosphere than you can imagine: horses, mules, oxen, wagons, costumes, buggies, bands, soldiers, carts, more horses, cowgirls, Indians, riding clubs, clowns, kids, more costumes, dust, and manure, lots of manure.

Dating from the 1930's, **Old Tucson** is an active movie lot complete with a sound studio. The public is welcome all year, even when movies are being filmed. The sets from famous westerns like **Rio Lobo** and **Arizona** are still there and make great photos. The kids will enjoy the magic shows, shooting gallery and rides. Staged gun fights by convincing professional stunt men are performed every hour.

Nothing can beat living the "cowboy way" to experience the flavor of

Facing Page: Rodeo action, La Fiesta de los Vaqueros, ©Edward McCain

131

the old west. Tucson is a center of world-class **"dude" ranches** which combine modern comforts with authentic western trimmings. Crusty wranglers and custom trail rides don't come cheap though, plan on spending at least $150 per day.

More realistic for many are **trail rides** of a few hours to get a "seat of the pants" feel for cowboy life. There are several excellent outfits that will provide a horse and a wrangler to take you through some desert scenery by horseback. Good fun and fine photo opportunities are guaranteed.

OLD TUCSON STUDIOS

Area of Town: West.
Map Reference: E 3.
Phone Numbers: Information 602-883-6457; Administration, 602-883-0100.
Directions: Take Speedway Blvd. west past I-10. It turns into a smaller road winding up into the mountains and changes names to Gates Pass Road. Follow this over the pass, down the other side to Kinney Road. Turn left at the stop sign and Old Tucson is on your left.
Best Time of Year: All year.
Best Time of Day: Late afternoon and sunset will be the best time for photographs. Ticket prices are discounted after 5:00 p.m..
Hours: 9:00 am until 9:00 pm. Closed Christmas and Thanksgiving.
Rules: Pets on leash.
Fees: Adults: $10.95, Children: $6.95. After 5:00 p.m., Adults: $6.95,
Children: $6:20.
Facilities: Restrooms, gift shop, restaurant.
Nearby Places of Interest: Arizona-Sonora Desert Museum; Gates Pass.

Comments:

This is the place to get the kid's pictures with "real" cowboys and settings. There are realistic "old" western buildings, mission churches, corrals and endless western photo opportunities. Photographs taken for personal use may be taken anywhere at Old Tucson. Professional photographers taking stock photos or photos for publication will be charged a fee. Please contact the public relations office for information. There are generally no restrictions on taking pictures during the filming of movies, but individual producers may ask that photos not be taken sometimes, particularly if major movie stars are involved.

𝖚𝖚𝖗𝖎𝖚𝖚𝖗 LA FIESTA DE LOS VAQUEROS

Area of Town: South Central.
Map Reference: F 6.
Phone Numbers: Rodeo tickets, 602-741-2233.
Directions: Go South on Stone Ave, until it joins 6th Ave., then continue
   south, past Ajo Way until you come to the **Pima County Rodeo**
   Grounds on the east side of 6th Ave If you are near I-10, take the 6th
   Ave. exit and go south on 6th past Ajo Way to the Rodeo Grounds.
Best Time of Year: Rodeo is held in late February.
Hours: Rodeo events are held from 1:15 pm until 4:30 pm daily.
Rules: See Comments.
Fees: Rodeo tickets are $5 to $6 .
Facilities: Restrooms, food and drink vendors.
Nearby Places of Interest: Mission San Xavier del Bac; "A" Mountain.

Comments:

There is enormous energy, color and excitement generated as the
cowboys and cowgirls compete in these death defying events. The
rodeo clowns make light of the danger but it is plain the bulls would love
to catch one of those cowboys they regularly throw.

You will have to photograph the events from your seat in the grandstand with a telephoto lens because the arena, the chutes, and certain
other areas are limited to press, media, and PRCA photographers with
credentials.

This is, however, a huge outdoor rodeo and you will have ample
opportunity to wander the Rodeo Grounds and contact riders, animals,
and activity to photograph. Remember, your safety and that of the riders
and animals is of primary importance.

𝖚𝖚𝖗𝖎𝖚𝖚𝖗𝖎𝖚𝖚𝖗 TUCSON RODEO PARADE

Area of Town: South Central.
Map Reference: E 6.
Phone Numbers: Grandstand tickets, 602-741-2233.
Directions: The Parade Route: Begins at intersection of Ajo Way and
   Park Ave., continues south on Park Ave. to Irvington, west on Irvington
   to 6th Ave., where it ends near the Rodeo Grounds.The grandstand
   seating is on Irvington near 6th. Traffic and parking are very difficult,
   so Sun Tran provides shuttle bus service from the parking lots of El
   Con and Tucson Malls to the Grandstand area. There is usually a map
   of the route in the morning paper.

Best Time of Year: The parade is Thursday of Rodeo Week in February.

Best Time of Day: The Parade begins at 9:00 am and is usually over by noon.

Nearby Places of Interest: Mission San Xavier del Bac; "A" Mountain; Barrio Historico; El Presidio Neighborhood.

Comments:

G randstand seating won't necessarily yield the best photos of the parade, but this is where the shuttle drops people off. You should probably be prepared to arrive early and walk along the parade route to scope out some good vantage points.

You might want to try to get down to the start at Ajo Way and Park Ave. very early and see the parade entries as they are getting organized in the early morning light. Remember, there will be practically no parking, blocked off streets and a certain amount of confusion, so take an adventurous spirit if you try this.

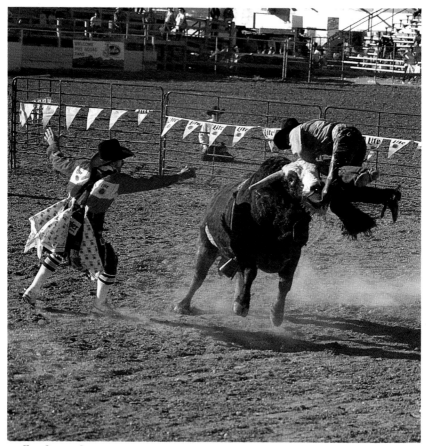

Bull rider in dire need of help, La Fiesta de los Vaqueros, © Edward McCain

⏣⏣⏣⏣⏣⏣⏣⏣ RILLITO DOWNS
Horse Racing

Area of Town: Central.

Map Reference: D 6.

Phone Number: 602-740-2690 (Pima County Parks & Recreation).

Directions: Easy to find at 1st Ave. and the Rillito River just south of River Rd.

Best Time of Year: Races held from November to March. Call for current year's race dates or check the sports page of the paper.

Hours: Open late morning, finishing up late afternoon; check the sports page for post time.

Rules: No pets.

Fees: They vary depending on the seating and who is running the track each particular year but they are cheap compared to going to the movies.

Facilities: Restaurant, parimuel betting.

Nearby Places of Interest: Tucson Mall.

Comments:

Spirited racing and a colorful crowd of folks from all over southern Arizona make this a fun afternoon. Both quarter horses and thorough-breds are raced and there is parimtuel betting with most of the betting quirks like trifectas to make things interesting. The Tucson Mall is nearby if someone in your party is not convinced this is a good time.

DUDE RANCHES

If you have the money and the time, staying at a dude ranch is the best way to relax and enjoy the best of the Old West without many of its discomforts. Being in the quiet desert environment 24 hours a day will provide an excellent opportunity to see and experience the desert.

These ranches are not motels! Each is geared to stays of at least several days and consider themselves "destination resorts" where you have come to enjoy their facilities. The rates reflect the full service and facilities they offer. The following is only a selection; check the Tucson Official Visitors Guide for complete listings and the latest information. (Available at 130 S. Scott, Tucson 85701, 602-624-1817; FAX 884-7804).

Tanque Verde Guest Ranch. Located on Tucson's east side this full-service guest ranch has it all. It is situated adjacent to the Rincon Mountains and Saguaro National Monument (East) so its trail rides are especially scenic. 14301 E. Speedway Blvd., Tucson, 602-296-6275.

Flying V Ranch. Next to the Loews Ventana Canyon Resort. Fine views with easy access to Ventana Canyon. Good hiking and bird watching. 6800 N. Flying V Guest Ranch Rd., Tucson, 602-299-4372.

White Stallion Ranch. Close to Tucson but isolated on its own 3,000 acre spread adjacent to Saguaro National Monument (West). 9251 W. Twin Peaks Rd., Tucson, 602-297-0252; 800-STALLION; FAX 602-744-2786.

Wild Horse Ranch Resort. Charming old ranch in the Tucson Mountains. 6801 N. Camino Verde, Tucson, 602-744-1012.

Elkhorn Ranch. Situated about 40 miles southwest of Tucson at the foot of the Baboquivari Mountains this old time ranch is isolated and has the feel of a genuine working cattle ranch, which it is. W. Elkhorn Ranch Rd., Robles, AZ., 602-822-1040.

Facing Page: Cowboy Sunset,
©Edward McCain

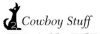 *Cowboy Stuff*

TRAIL RIDES

If you want the old West experience without the expense and commitment of going to a dude ranch the next best thing is a trail ride. The outfits listed below provide manageable horses and colorful wranglers. They also offer a wide variety of activities like cookouts, moonlight or sunset rides and private parties. Even for a simple trail ride call ahead for reservations. Expect to pay about $12.00 per hour, longer rides will probably be a little less per hour. Check on the rates when you call for reservations. Excellent photo opportunities.

Pusch Ridge Stables. This outfit has a great location at the base of Pusch Ridge and on the edge of Catalina State Park. 11220 N. Oracle Rd., Tucson, 602-297-6908.

El Conquistador Stables. Located at the El Conquistador Resort it shares the same great riding country with Pusch Ridge Stables. 10000 N. Oracle Rd., Tucson, 602-742-4200.

Bar J Ranch. Features a central location. 3131 N Pantano Rd., Tucson, 886-7488..

Pantano Stables. Near Saguaro National Monument (East). 4450 S. Houghton Rd., Tucson, 602-298-9076.

Desert-High Country. Features the saguaro forests of the adjacent Saguaro National Monument (West) in the Tucson Mountains. 6501 W. Ina Rd, Tucson, 602-744-3789

There are several mid-winter opportunities to catch the excitement and color of a major bicycle event. **El Tour de Tucson** is a benefit ride with riders entering 111-mile, 75-mile, 50-mile and 25-mile courses. Top racers from around the country come to compete in the 111-mile course, but riders of every level of skill, conditioning and commitment enter the shorter courses. The "Tour" starts early in the morning downtown; be there to take photos of sleek brightly clad athletes in rainbow mirror sunglasses in great early morning light.

The **Tour of the Tucson Mountains** is not as big an event as El Tour de Tucson but it traverses the saguaro-clad Tucson Mountains and also provides fine viewing and photo opportunities.

If you are interested in bicycle racing you won't want to miss **La Vuelta de Bisbee**, the most important bicycle race in Arizona. Held yearly in picturesque Bisbee with its steep narrow streets and unique setting and architecture, it presents fantastic photo opportunities.

Photo Tips: Conveying the essence of bicycle racing means capturing the impression of speed. A photo of a bicycle racer caught in a moment which is thrilling to a spectator may lose the excitement because the camera freezes the motion. There are several ways to get an image that preserves the excitement of the moment.

"Panning" is a technique in which you hold the camera on the subject as it moves and press the shutter while the camera is still moving. The subject will be frozen but the background will be blurred. This is the easiest method because you do not have to change any camera settings and it can be done with even the simplest camera.

Trickier, but sometimes very effective, is simply using a **slow shutter speed** if your camera is adjustable. If your camera has a shutter priority mode set the shutter for 1/30th or less. If it only has an aperture priority mode choose a small aperture which will cause the camera to select a slow shutter speed. Hold the camera stationary and steady as the subject moves by and you will get a blurred image which conveys motion of the subject with the background relatively visible but perhaps a little blurred from the low shutter speed if you hand held the camera. If you elect to experiment with this method be sure you take some shots with a higher shutter speed (at least 1/125) to freeze the action so you have some acceptable images recording the event to take home.

EL TOUR DE TUCSON

Area of Town: All over; begins and ends downtown.
Phone Number: 602-745-2033.
Directions: The race begins and ends downtown at the intersection of Congress Street and Granada Ave., two blocks east of I-10 at the Congress Street exit. The current route will be published in the newspaper.
Best Time of Year: Race is held in November.
Hours: The tour begins at 7:00 am.
Rules: Stay out of the way of the racers; cooperate with race officials.
Fees: None.
Facilities: There are restaurants, stores, and hotels downtown.
Nearby Places of Interest: "A" Mountain; Saguaro National Monument (West).

Comments:

You will be able to view the tour from anywhere along the 100 mile route that runs around the city and county, through all kinds of terrain and neighborhoods. The route will be published in the newspaper. The most excitement will be downtown at the start and the end of the race.

TOUR OF TUCSON MOUNTAINS

Area of Town: West.
Map Reference: B-F, 1-5.
Directions: The beginning and end of the ride are at the Main Gate of the University of Arizona campus. This is at the intersection of Park Ave. and University Blvd.
Best Time of Year: The event is held in April.
Best Time of Day: The light will be best around the 8:00 am starting time.
Hours: Starts at 8:00 am.
Rules: Stay out of the way of the racers; cooperate with race officials.
Fees: None.
Facilities: There are restrooms and restaurants in the Student Union building on campus, and restaurants and stores on University Blvd, near the Main Gate.
Nearby Places of Interest: University of Arizona; the Center for Creative Photography is on the north side of the campus.

Comments:

The route of this ride goes through downtown, out Ajo Way and around the Tucson Mountains. You might enjoy watching and photographing the riders from some point on the west side of the mountains in the cactus forest. Check the newspaper for a map of the route the day before.

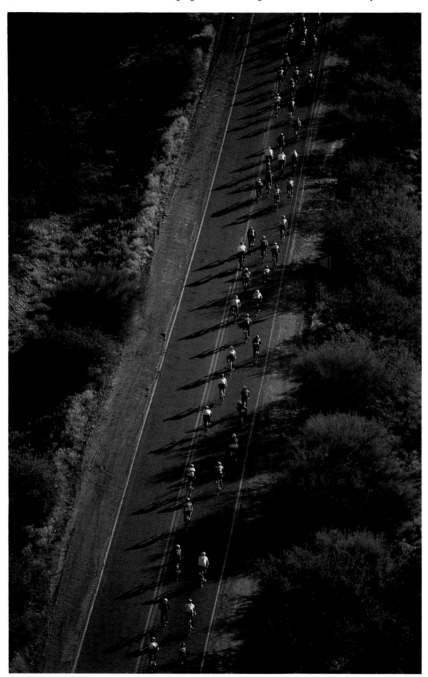

El Tour de Tucson, ©*Edward McCain*

F or experiencing and photographing color, just about nothing beats going to a mass balloon rise. It is an intense experience to walk around in the cold rarefied early morning air surrounded by great billowing forms of richly hued balloon cloth catching the light on the surface and glowing from within. Everyone feels the excitement and anticipation of pure simple flight.

The Old Pueblo Balloon Classic is the big balloon event of the year with as many as a hundred balloons and thousands of people attending. The excitement starts before dawn as the participants ready their craft amid the hurly burly of tens of thousands of spectators. Just after dawn the brilliant armada takes off with only a low whooshing of gas heaters as they heat the envelope of air in the balloon.

The **Balloon Glo** held in December on the University of Arizona campus lights up the balloons in the evening for a romantic view of them looking like so many giant paper lanterns in the night. The balloons lift off the next morning.

Balloon Rides

T he best way to experience ballooning is to take a ride. There are usually outfits which can arrange rides. Expect to pay about $110 per person for an hour and a half long ride. As of this writing only one of the several companies that has offered this service recently is still active in Tucson. **Southern Arizona Balloon Excursions** (602-624-3599) is available to arrange rides by reservation. Try the yellow pages for others which may become available. The concierge at one of the fancy hotels like the Ventana or La Paloma resorts may also have a line on available services.

Winter is the ballooning season and they take off at the crack of dawn. This is a once in a lifetime photo opportunity.

Photo Tips: Besides scenic shots from the balloon you may be able to capture the excitement of the people in the gondola itself. It is surprising how close some lenses will focus, especially wide angle ones. Even a standard 50mm lens should focus down to a few feet.

OLD PUEBLO BALLOON CLASSIC

Area of Town: Southwest.
Map Reference: F 5.
Phone Number: 602-883-7504.
Directions: From I-10, take the I-19 exit and go south to the Valencia Road exit. Go west on Valencia Road until the traffic and the signs direct you to the balloon grounds and parking.
Best Time of Year: Held in February.
Best Time of Day: The balloons go up at sunrise, see Appendix Two.
Rules: No pets please.
Fees: Varies, call the number above.
Facilities: Restrooms.
Nearby Places of Interest: San Xavier del Bac Mission.

Comments:

This is a very popular event in Tucson; plan on being up very early to join in the traffic. Have your coffee and donuts with you for when you start to fade later in the morning.

Photo tips. For the predawn activity you may need fast film and/or a tripod. Of course, the most dramatic colors won't appear until the sun hits the balloons. When it does, a film no faster than 200 ISO will produce the best photographs. The slower the film the better the color saturation.

Don't forget that a little blur caused by movement in a scene like this can be appealing. Experiment by using a slower shutter speed to capture this effect.

BALLOON GLO

Area of Town: Central.

Map Reference: E 7; see also map on page 124.

Phone: 602-624-1889 (Tucson Visitors Bureau).

Directions: The Balloon Glo is held on the central mall of the University of Arizona campus. Park at one of the lots just west of the main gate.

Best Time of Year: The Balloon Glo is held in December.

Hours: Festivities start at dusk on Friday night, continuing until 8:00 pm. The balloons lift off around sunrise on Saturday morning.

Rules: No dogs.

Fees: None..

Facilities: Restrooms and restaurants in the Student Union Building. There are more restaurants on University Blvd. to the west of campus and on Speedway to the north, all within walking distance.

Nearby Places of Interest: Arizona State Museum; Arizona Heritage Museum.

Comments:

This is a unique opportunity to see the balloons in juxtaposition with the campus buildings. Also, the campus itself is well worth seeing. Besides the museums, the desert landscaping contains many excellent specimens which are often marked for identification. Visit the **Flandrau Planetarium** and the **Center for Creative Photography**.

Photo Tips: This may be one of the few times you get to use Kodak's 1000 speed film to full advantage. The results are a little grainy but the colors are very good and it has an appealing texture when shot in an evening lighting situation. 400 speed might also yield good results depending on your camera. Remember for best results you do not want to shoot with film this fast in the daylight because the contrast will be too high and the colors disappointing.

Facing Page: Balloon Glo, University of Arizona, ©Randy Prentice

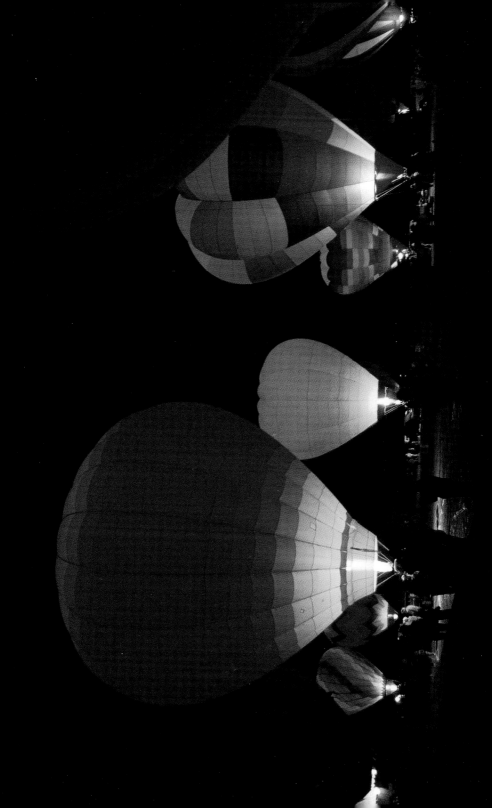

Tucson contains a rich diversity of people who have chosen to make the desert home. **"Anglos"** from every state and nation call Tucson home and yet many maintain their cultural roots which they proudly display at events like **"Tucson Meet Yourself."** The **Hispanic** community has a deep and constant identity both in Tucson and with families in Mexico. **Native Americans** retain their sovereignty on the reservation but also participate actively in Tucson community life. **African-American** Tucsonans have a cohesive sense of community and have contributed many public leaders to Tucson. The **Chinese** community has prospered since its trials in territorial Arizona. Other Asian peoples like **Vietnamese** and **Thais** have joined the Chinese, especially in the post Vietnam War era. The University of Arizona has drawn a large **Arab** student body in part due to its Arid Lands Study Program.

Throw in about **30,000** fun-loving **undergraduate students** from the University of Arizona, a bunch of **airmen** and **airwomen** from Davis-Monthan Air Force Base, some visiting **cowboys** and **cowgirls** from all over southern Arizona, lots of **aging hippies**, a big dollop of **snow birds**, **tons of tourists** from all over the world, and a constant stream of **people from Mexico** and you have quite a mix.

Fortunately Tucson provides many opportunities for its diverse population to interact and enjoy each other. The **Rodeo Parade** and **La Fiesta de los Vaqueros** emphasise Tucson's ranching roots. The **Fourth Ave. Street Fair** showcases the crafts of artisans from all over the west and brings out folks from every part of the community. The **Tucson Gem and Mineral Show** not only brings out many Tucsonans, but draws an amazing variety of people from around the world who come here every year to do business and renew business contacts and friendships.

Tucson Meet Yourself always provides surprises as you find out the tasty variety of food Tucson's different ethnic groups produce. **Downtown Saturday Night** gives the hip and the unhip a chance to share the crowded sidewalks for an evening in the **Arts District**.

FOURTH AVENUE STREET FAIR

Area of Town: Central.

Map Reference: E 6.

Phone Number: 800-933-2477; 602-624-5004; FAX 602-624-5933.

Directions: Take Fourth Avenue south from Speedway and you'll run into the Fair before you know it. Parking is problematic and you'll have to walk a few blocks from wherever you are lucky enough to find a spot.

Best Time of Year: The Fair is held the first or second week in December and again the first week in April. Check the newspaper or call for current dates.

Best Time of Day: By early afternoon the sun is toasty and the street is crowded. If you want less crowding, come on Friday afternoon.

Hours: Friday noon to dark; Saturday & Sunday 9:00 am to dark.

Rules: Pets on leash.

Fees: None.

Facilities: Food & craft vendors, restrooms.

Nearby Places of Interest: University of Arizona; El Presidio Neighborhood.

Comments:

Fourth Avenue retains its atmosphere from the hippy days when some of the current businesses were started. There are all kinds of fun shops here and it is definitely worth a stroll even when the Fair is not on. From prosaic services like furniture refinishing to fine jewelry design there are dozens of shops to explore along the avenue.

The Fair brings artisans from all over the West. Several hundred booths offer everything from good karma to beef jerky. There are plenty of food vendors offering corn on the cob, egg rolls, burgers, pizza, ribs, vegetarian food, you name it.

But, the people are the attraction. Good street musicians vie with jugglers and sword swallowers for the crowd's attention. The crowd itself is something to see. Sikhs and students, babes and bikers, young and old, the diverse crowd migrates up and down the avenue, taking it all in.

Photo tips: Take a long lens for good shots of the crowd. Be aware of the background, a great image may be ruined because of distractions behind the subject. Remember the street entertainers make their living from passing the hat so toss in something if you take a photo.

▨▨▨ TUCSON GEM & MINERAL SHOW

Area of Town: Downtown.

Map Reference: E 6.

Phone Number: 791-4266 (Tucson Convention Center).

Directions: Public portion of the show is located in the Tucson Convention Center, downtown. The wholesale part of the show is held in motels all over town but the biggest concentration is on the frontage road on the west side of I-10 at Congress St.

Best Time of Year: Held in the first two weeks of February.

Best Time of Day: All day.

Hours: The activities outside the convention center are daytime only. The hours at the public show at the Tucson Convention Center are Thursday & Friday 10:00 am to 7:00 pm; Saturday 10:00 am to 6:30 pm; Sunday 10:00 am to 5:00 pm.

Rules: Some of the vendors sell wholesale only.

Fees: None for the wholesale shows in the motels; the Community Center will charge about $3.00 for the public show.

Facilities: Restrooms, snack bars.

Nearby Places of Interest: Barrio Historico; El Presidio Neighborhood; "A" Mountain.

Comments:

This is not your average street fair or swap meet. Gem and mineral dealers from all over the United States, India, Russia, Switzerland, South Africa, Brazil and many other countries use the Gem and Mineral Show as a way to sell wholesale and to make contacts in their business.

The most interesting part of the show is the chaotic wholesale market which is strewn along the I-10 frontage road just west of downtown. Just get off the freeway at Congress, head down the west frontage road and you can't miss it. Incidentally although the focus is wholesale there are a number of dealers who sell retail.

Coming across a perfect six-foot dinosaur skeleton mounted on the wall at a Motel 6 is strangely disconcerting. Having to edge your way around an elegant piece of amethyst as big as a couch to get a cup of coffee in the lobby is similarly odd.

The public show in the Community Center is much more organized. Besides offering gems and minerals there are sales of rock cutting and polishing hardware and an amazing variety of "findings" to make jewelry. Usually there will be a display of famous diamonds or other precious stones loaned from somewhere like the Smithsonian Institute in Washington, DC.

Facing Page: 4th Avenue Street Fair, ©Edward McCain

TUCSON MEET YOURSELF

Area of Town: Downtown.
Map Reference: E 6.
Phone Number: 602-621-3392.
Directions: Downtown in El Presidio Park, behind the Old Courthouse. See map on page 118.
Best Time of Year: Held in Mid-October.
Best Time of Day: Late morning through dinner time.
Hours: Friday 6:00 pm to 10:00 pm; Saturday noon to 10:00 pm; Sunday 1:00 pm to sundown.
Rules: Pets on leash.
Fees: None.
Facilities: Restrooms, lots of food vendors.
Nearby Places of Interest: Barrio Historico; El Presidio Neighborhood; "A" Mountain.

Comments:

Affectionately known to locals as "Tucson Eat Yourself" this is a truly fun community event. Food vendors from dozens of community organizations offer mountains of great chow.

Besides the food there are concerts, folk dancing, cowboy story telling and other events for your entertainment. This is a good chance to do the El Presidio tour and walk off a few calories at the same time.

There is also a craft area where one and all, especially kids, can get instructions in traditional crafts. On Saturday, a Lowrider Show and a Costume Paseo (fashion parade) are annual events.

𝕊𝕌ℝ𝕊𝕌ℝ𝕊𝕌ℝ MARIACHI CONFERENCE

Area of Town: Downtown.

Map Reference: E 6.

Phone Number: 602-884-9920 (La Frontera Center, the sponsor); Concerts tickets 791-4266.

Directions: La Fiesta de Garibaldi is in Armory Park, two blocks south of Broadway on 6th Ave. Los Concerts Espectacular are held at the Tucson Convention Center, downtown.

Best Time of Year: The conference is held four days in April.

Best Time of Day: La Fiesta de Garibaldi is most pleasant in late afternoon and evening.

Hours: Los Espectacular Concerts are held at 7:30 pm on Friday night, and 2:00 pm on Saturday afternoon. La Fiesta de Garibaldi is held in Armory Park on Saturday from 10:00 am to 10:00 pm.

Rules: Pets on leash, actually it's pretty crowded at the park and everyone would probably be more comfortable without the pooch.

Fees: The tickets to the Concerts are $10, $25, $50 (Remember this is a benefit for a good cause).The Fiesta de Garibaldi in the park is free.

Facilities: There are restrooms in the Community Center and at Armory Park. The Fiesta de Garibaldi has food booths for some of the most authentic Mexican food north of the border.

Nearby Places of Interest: Barrio Historico; El Presidio Neighborhood.

Comments:

The Mariachi Conference is an international gathering of mariachi bands. The first three days are professional workshops for the musicians. Los Concerts Espectacular are the grand finale of the Conference and provide the best in Mariachi music for the true fan. The concerts almost always include performances by Linda Ronstadt and the best Mariachi bands from Mexico City, Los Angeles and the rest of the United States and Mexico.

La Fiesta de Garibaldi in Armory Park is where the really good people watching is. Bands play all day and evening, and there are food booths for creating an onsite picnic. The atmosphere is relaxed and delightfully international.

This entire event is a fundraiser for La Frontera, a mental health and rehabilitation facility for substance abuse.

Tucson sits in the middle of some of the most beautiful and diverse country in the world. From dry, creosote-covered valleys to forested 9,000-foot mountains, there is an enormous amount of country to explore. Besides the natural beauty, there are numerous cultural aspects worthy of a trip, from the ancient Native American sites to the latest space-age astronomy of Kitt Peak National Observatory.

Obviously, if you are in town for a week you cannot do all these day trips. Even if you had the time, some may not appeal. Look them over and you'll find something that will lure you out of town for a day.

Biosphere 2, located about 25 miles north of town, is a fascinating look at a controversial science experiment. The main facility is an enormous greenhouse housing several distinct environments from the tropical to deep sea. Several scientists have spent years in the sealed environment to find out how well the environment can sustain itself.

Kitt Peak is a pleasant drive and the setting of the National Observatory at almost 7,000 feet is dramatic. The science is well explained in tours. The vistas of the **Tohono O'Odham** Reservation are sweeping.

The village of **Arivaca** is set in rolling hills, with the green swath of **Arivaca Creek** running through it. Next to the village **Buenos Aires National Wildlife Refuge** offers views of exotic birdlife in the wetlands along the creek.

Tubac and nearby **Tumacacori National Monument** are a nice change after the city traffic of Tucson. They are quiet country places with a lot to offer to those interested in art and southwest history.

Nogales, Sonora is a 90-minute drive south of Tucson on I-19, but the cultural trip is into another world.

Empire-Cienega Resource Conservation Area is an enormous piece of southern Arizona which has been dedicated for conservation. It includes hilly ranch country and, at its heart, a rare area of wetlands which is home to numerous species of threatened plant and animal.

Kartchner Caverns State Park is included even though it will not open until 1994 or 1995. This jewel of a cave has formations which are the talk of the caving world. The story of its discovery and the years of secrecy surrounding it is fascinating.

Facing Page Top left: Downtown Tucson
Top right: Old Pima County Courthouse
Bottom left: Arizona State Office Building at Main & Congress
Bottom right: Restored Owl's Club, Main near Franklin

The beautiful rolling hills of **Sonoita** and **Patagonia** are the dream places in southern Arizona. More than one harried businessperson, lawyer or doctor has said "the hell with it" and moved down here to write a book.

The **San Pedro Riparian Conservation Area** is like the Buenos Aires NWR in that it is huge with no dramatic focal point other than the meandering San Pedro River. Instead it exists to preserve species which need the space and the quiet which predominates here.

The **Amerind Foundation** is an example of science in the bygone day. In the 1800's and early 1900's it was not uncommon for rich men and women to adopt an area of science and apply their time and money to advancing it. The Amerind Foundation museum contains the Native American artifacts and art collection of William Shirley Fulton who pursued a life-long passion for archaeology and anthropology in the American Southwest. The collection is well worth seeing.

Ramsey Canyon is very different from the San Pedro Riparian Area and Buenos Aires NWR, although it too was created to preserve threatened species. Instead of a huge amorphous area, this preserve is confined to a single canyon and only limited numbers of visitors are allowed. If you are lucky enough to visit you will find an extraordinary place to view unusual plants and birds, especially hummingbirds.

Cochise Stronghold is what southern Arizona is all about -- beautiful, rugged and with a rich history. It is easy to drive to but it is not easy to fully experience its mystery unless you are willing to invest some time and energy hiking.

Tombstone and Bisbee are part of the "Old West." Tombstone is a tourist town with honest credentials. Bisbee was a working mining town for many years. Set in the rugged canyons of the Mule Mountains it is a living history of the lives of the miners and their families who made the desert outpost home.

Chiricahua National Monument was established to protect the most unbelievable fairyland of rock statuary you can imagine. Quiet paths wind for miles among the rhyolite towers. But, this is one natural area you can enjoy without a lot of walking if you prefer the car. There are numerous roadside vistas available to enjoy nature's handiwork.

Facing Page: Biosphere 2 during "Closure Party," ©Edward McCain

BIOSPHERE 2

Area Of Town: 25 miles north.

Phone Number: 602-825-6200 or 825-6222.

Map Reference: T 5.

Directions: Biosphere 2 is twenty miles north of the intersections of Oracle Rd. and Ina Rd. in Tucson. Drive north on Oracle Rd. for 16 miles and then bear right at Oracle Junction onto Highway 77. From here you drive 6 miles to the well marked turn-off on the right. Then it is just 2 more miles to the parking lot.

Best Times Of Year: It will be hot in the summer and there is a fair amount of walking on the tours.

Hours: 8:00 am to 6:30 pm in the summer, and 8:00 am to 5:30 pm in the winter.

Rules: No dogs, no picnics.

Fees: Adults, $12.95; seniors, $10.95; children up to 17 years, $6.00; children 4 years and under, free.

Facilities: Restrooms, restaurant, snackbars, gift shops, hotel accommodations, wheelchair and stroller rentals.

Nearby Places Of Interest: Catalina State Park.

Comments:

Biosphere 2 is an educational roadside attraction, and an environmental research facility. A huge, graceful greenhouse houses several carefully constructed ecosystems: tropical rainforest, savannah, marsh, 25-foot deep ocean, desert, an intensive agriculture area, and a human habitat. One ongoing experiment has been housing several scientists in the enclosed environments for years at a time.

Because this is a research facility, the Biosphere building is completely sealed off in order to maintain the air, water, nutrient and waste environment. Visitors cannot enter this building, but you can walk around outside and look in. There is also an underwater viewing area in the ocean environment. The various ecosystems are reconstructed on a smaller scale in another building where visitors can take a guided tour. There is an orientation center and plenty of tour guides to tell you about the current studies being done, and all about how Biosphere 2 works.

For the kids, there is a BioFair with numerous hands-on scientific demonstrations like a giant gyroscope and a walk-through maze.

The entire tour, if you go all the way around the building, is a mile long. It will be hot in summer. The views out over the desert are great because the facility is built on a hilltop just north of the Santa Catalina Mountains.

To drive out to Biosphere 2, tour the facility, and have lunch in the restaurant will take about 4 or 5 hours. As this is an expensive trip, be sure to allow enough time to enjoy yourself and learn everything there is to learn. Remember, much of this tour is walking outside, so go on a nice day.

KITT PEAK

Area Of Town: 50 miles west.
Map Reference: W 2.
Phone Number: 602-325-9200.
Directions: Take I-10 to I-19 and go south and exit on Ajo Way Head west on Ajo (Hwy. 86) for about 36 miles to the Kitt Peak Rd. (Hwy. 386) and follow it for 13 miles. Allow 90 minutes for the drive.
Best Time Of Year: All year.
Hours: 9:00 am to 4:00 pm everyday except Thanksgiving, Christmas Eve Day, Christmas Day and New Years Day. Tours at 11:00 am, 1:00 pm and 2:30 pm.
Rules: Pets on a leash; visitors strictly limited to the public areas.
Fees: None; $2.00 suggested donation per person.
Facilities: Picnic area; restrooms; soda machines; gift shop; no food or gas.
Nearby Places Of Interest: Sells, the capital of the Tohono O'Odham Nation is located on Hwy. 86 about 14 miles west of the turnoff to Kitt Peak.

Comments:

This is one of the most visually striking sights you will ever see. Enourmous white observatory domes dot the skyline of a jagged granite mountain range, set off against the bluest sky imaginable. The paths among the facilities are in a quiet setting of oak groves and a new view reveals itself at every turn. The quiet is planned, by the way, as many workers sleep in the dormitories by day after a night of star gazing.

Do not forget to get snacks and gas at the store you pass at Three Points, there is none past there. But, there is a good Visitors Center with interpretive exhibits and a gift shop featuring astronomy oriented items as well as Tohono O'Odham crafts.

Kitt Peak Road is a mountain road, but a lot better than the Mt. Lemmon highway. It is popular as a workout for hard-core bicyclists.

Kitt Peak at an altitude of 6,875 feet is the highest point in the **Quinlin Mountains**. All the land in and around the range is on the **Tohono O'Odham Reservation**. The observatory site is leased by the tribe to a consortium of universities operating as the **National Optical Astronomy Observatories**. Located to the south, about 15 miles north of the border with Mexico, is **Baboquivari Peak**, 7,740 feet.

Arivaca figured in the history of the Spanish missionary efforts and **Father Kino** included it on his map of Primeria Alta in 1695. The present town dates from mining days in the mid 1800's when silver was found nearby. There is a walking tour of the townsite and you can pick up a map for it at the store or restaurant.

The distinctive feature of Arivaca is the natural wetlands or "**cienega**" (Spanish for hundred waters) along the perennial **Arivaca Creek**. Now part of Buenos Aires National Wildlife Refuge these wet green areas seem incongruous in their arid desert setting. They support huge cottonwood trees and attract many species of birds, animals and amphibians. Flowers and all manner of greenery not seen in the desert are lush here.

The wetlands are easy to enjoy thanks to a dry trail constructed around it. The trail head is just south of town on the Ruby Rd. The trail is short, flat and pleasant.

Three miles west of town on the **Sasabe Rd.** (Hwy. 386) is the **Arivaca Creek Trailhead**. The creek is crowned with cottonwoods, some two hundred years old and ten feet in diameter. The area is home to coatimundis and birds which the refuge literature describes as "neotropical".

Ruby Rd. is recommended by the locals as a good loop back to the interstate. It does have much to recommend it from the standpoint of scenery and history but the road itself is pure hell, rough and twisting, up and down, for seemingly endless miles after the Arivaca Lake turnoff.

If you are interested in a loop back to Tucson you might consider going west on Sasabe Rd. (Hwy. 386, a good road paved with gravel) through the Buenos Aires National Wildlife Refuge and then taking 286 and 86 back to Tucson. Allow about 2 hours to return this way. See map on page 95.

Day Trips

TUBAC

Area of Town: 50 miles south.

Map Reference: Y4.

Phone Number: 602-398-2252 (Tubac Presidio State Historical Park);
602-398-2371 (Tubac Center of the Arts).

Directions: I-10 to I-19 south to exit 34, about 40 miles (65 kilometers).

Best Time of Year: All year; in February you can catch the Tubac
Festival of Arts, with many artisans and artists displaying their wares
in addition to the usual shops and galleries.

Best Time of Day: Go early to catch the good light on the mission at
nearby Tumacacori and then visit Tubac, or vica versa, catching the
late light at Tumacacori.

Hours: The shops are generally open 10:00 am to 5:00 pm; Tubac Presidio
State Historical Park hours are 8:00 am to 5:00 pm, closed Christmas
Day only.

Rules: Spend a lot of money.

Fees: $2.00 entry fee for the state park.

Facilities: Shops, restaurants; picnic area.

Nearby Places of Interest: Tumacacori National Monument, Nogales.

Comments:

History: In the **mid 1500's** several Spanish expeditions tramped back
and forth across Arizona looking for the rich hordes of gold they had
found in Mexico and South America. Disappointed by cities of gold which
turned out to be cities of mud, Spanish interest in the area dimmed,
leaving only a few Jesuits to contribute martyrs to missionary lore through
the **1600's** and early **1700's**.

When the Spanish came, Southern Arizona was heavily populated by
Pima, **Tohono O'Odham** (fka Papago) and **Sobaipuri** Indians. They
lived in numerous villages along the flowing rivers of that day, especially
the Santa Cruz River which runs north from Mexico through the heart of
Southern Arizona. The Spanish introduced cattle, horses and Christianity
and established military presidios in several places, including Tubac and
Tucson. The Indians controlled their lands although the Spanish organized united military expeditions against the **Apaches** and others from
time to time using thousands of Pima and Sobaipuri braves as allies.

Then, in **1736**, a **Yaqui** Indian made a rich silver find at a place called
Arizonac by the Spanish, just southwest of what is now Nogales. The
name **Arizonac** may derive either from the Tohono O'Odham words ali
shonak (little spring) or the Basque words arritza onac (good or valuable
rocky place) or aritz onac (good or valuable oaks).

The find was so rich, chunks of silver just laying around on the surface, that there was lengthy litigation over whether it was treasure (50% went to the king) or a mine (20% to the king). Arizonac came to be synonymous for quick riches and many prospectors and settlers moved north.

The Pima Indians who occupied much of southern Arizona resisted the new settlers and the **Pima Revolt of 1751** pushed the Spanish out. This resulted in a military fort, a Presidio, being constructed in 1753 at what is now Tubac, although it was first called **San Ignacio**. A mission was established as well. Within a short time there were several hundred residents.

The Presidio was moved north to Tucson in **1776**, leaving the residents without protection from hostile Indians and the settlement declined. Eventually many of the friendly Indians fell victim to epidemics

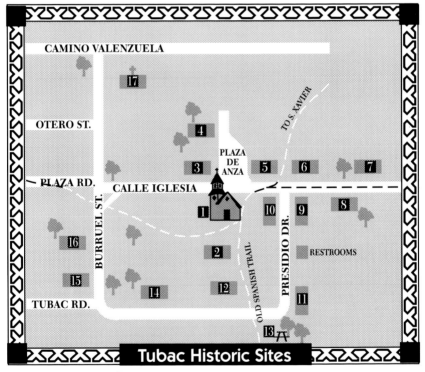

1. St. Ann's Church
2. Old Tubac Schoolhouse
3. Pennington House
4. Pedro Herreras House
5. Lowe House
6. Territorial House/East House
7. Ysidro Otero House
8. Brownell House
9. Espinoza House
10. Tubac Presidio State Park Museum
11. Rojas House
12. Otero Hall
13. Tubac Presidio State Historic Park Picnic Ground
14. Sabori House, 1885-1890
15. Old Garrett Stable
16. Garret House
17. "Cemetery"

Walking distance is 0.9 miles.

of European diseases and the predation of raiding Apaches after Spanish troops were withdrawn with Mexican independence in **1821**. Still, Tubac survived and in **1848** was described by travelers as being in excellent condition. But in **1849** a calamity, probably an attack by **Apaches**, destroyed the mission. Travelers in 1849 described the mission as being roofless and in poor repair. In the underground exhibit at the State Park you can observe a layer of ash resulting from a massive fire of that period.

There is a more romantic version of Tubac's destruction as well. According to this legend a young man in charge of maintenance at the mission was in love with a local señorita. She did not reciprocate his feelings and chose instead to marry a soldier in the mission. During the ceremony the jilted young man ascended the bell tower and began to ring out the Song of the Dead on the mission bell. The frightened congregation fled the building just as lightning struck the mission. After this tragedy it was abandoned.

Touring Tubac: It is easy to get confused in this rambling little town but there are interesting shops and restaurants at every turn. To get a feel for the town's Hispanic heritage visit the **cemetery** with memorials going back many years and the numerous piles of river stones placed to protect the graves from coyotes. **Tubac Presidio State Historical Park** features an interesting museum and interpretive displays of the archaeology that has been accomplished there.

In the area of the state park there are remains of buildings from Arizona's **territorial days**. Several of the small adobe and tin-roofed buildings reminiscent of this period are located here.

TUMACACORI

Area of Town: 40 miles south.
Map Reference: Y4.
Phone Number: 602-398-2341 (Tumacacori National Monument).
Directions: I-10 to I-19 south to exit 34, about 40 miles (65 kilometers).
Best Time of Year: All year; **Tumacacori Festival** on the first Sunday in December.
Best Time of Day: Early and late for the best light.
Hours: The grounds are open 24 hours. The interior of the mission and the museum are open 8:00 am to 5:00 pm every day except Christmas and Thanksgiving.
Rules: Be careful for your own safety on the uneven walks and in the low doorways.
Fees: $2.00 per person over 16 and under 62.
Facilities: Restrooms; book shop; picnic area.

Nearby Places of Interest: Tubac; Nogales.

Comments:

P ima Indians had long maintained small farming villages along this stretch of the Santa Cruz River before the coming of the Spanish. **Father Kino** first visited this site in **1691**. As was his custom, he introduced cattle, sheep and horses to the Indians, in addition to the tenets of the Holy Roman Catholic Church. In **1699** he wrote in his diary of a visit to Tumacacori:

Around 3 in the afternoon we began to travel [from **Guevavi** *in the south] the 5 leagues [about 12 miles] to* **San Cayetano** *(Tumacacori), arriving at nightfall. Their native governor met us a league from the village. Crosses and arches were set up along the way. The roads were clean, and they had built an earthen-roofed adobe house, where we slept. I said mass the following day.*

On the 28th we rested for half a day. The native governor presented his own little son for Father Visitor [Father Kino's Jesuit superior] to baptize, and he was named Ignacio. Another male child was presented for me to baptize, and he was named Antonio. Some 40 Indians from farther west came over to greet us. The local alcalde showed us their harvest of the maize that had been planted for the village and the Father they await. Father Visitor remarked that in all his life he had never seen such large ears of maize with such beautiful kernels. We counted over 800 kernels on some of the ears. That afternoon, we traveled 6 leagues [about 15 miles] to the watering place after which this river [the Santa Cruz] usually disappears, and flows 8 leagues [about 20 miles] underground to a point near **San Xavier del Bac***.*

Mission San Jose de Tumacacori was called **San Cayetano** until **1753** when the mission was moved to the west side of the river at the same time the Presidio at Tubac was built. The church that you see here now was started in **1800** by Franciscan missionaries who replaced the Jesuits after they were expelled from the New World in 1767. In **1828** all European born priests were expelled upon Mexican independence and Tumacacori deteriorated and was abandoned after **Apaches raids** in **1848**.

The church is a **photographer's dream**. It does not seem to have a bad angle and the possibilities are endless. From the formal front view to the sinuous walls in the rear the textures and light are a delight.

Day Trips

Area of Town: 60 miles south.

Map Reference: Z5.

Phone Number: 602-287-3685 (Nogales-Santa Cruz Chamber of Commerce).

Directions: I-10 to I-19 to exit 4.

Best Time of Year: All year; avoid midday in the summer.

Best Time of Day: All day except when it is hot in the summer. Although Nogales is at about 5,000 feet elevation, it will still be too hot for comfort in midday.

Hours: Generally the shops will be open from about 9:00 am to dusk but some may be closed for siesta in the early afternoon.

Rules: Be courteous to all officials, they are not impressed that you are an American. Do not drive without Mexican **insurance** in Nogales Sonora, you may end up in jail if you have an accident. Do not try to bring back drugs which require a prescription in the U.S. unless you have the prescription with you. **No visa** is required to cross the border just to shop in Nogales, Sonora. If you are going **past Nogales** you need a car permit which should be arranged in Tucson or Nogales at a Mexican insurance company to avoid a long delay in Mexico! You will also **need a visa to go further south** than Nogales. To get one you will need proof of citizenship, a birth certificate, voter registration card or passport are acceptable but a drivers license is not. You can bring back $400 worth of goods including one quart of liquor without paying duty.

Fees: None.

Facilities: Many stores and restaurants.

Nearby Places of Interest: Tumacacori National Monument; Tubac; Patagonia.

Comments:

There are actually two towns named Nogales on the border, one on each side. Most people view the Arizona town only as a place to park, but actually it has an interesting history of its own. The **Pimeria Alta Historical Society Museum** has instructive exhibits of photos and artifacts. Hours are 9:00 am to 5:00 pm Monday through Friday, Saturday 10:00 am to 4:00 pm and Sunday 1:00 pm to 5:00 pm. No entrance fee. The phone is 602-287-4621.

Most people do not drive into Nogales, Sonora. The streets are crowded and narrow. The Mexican drivers can be a little aggressive and if you have an accident Mexican law presumes you are guilty until proven

Facing Page: Mission San Jose de Tumacacori

innocent. So, **park on the US side** and walk over, it's only a couple of blocks. The best bet is to park in one of the guarded lots near the McDonald's just west of the border crossing (see map).

Walking around the shopping district is no problem. It is a little confusing but compact and manageable. To see the rest of the town I'd suggest a taxi. Otherwise you may feel pretty uncomfortable wandering around neighborhoods where tourists are not too welcome. I don't mean the Mexicans are not very friendly, they are, but how would you like some German or Japanese tourists staring in your yard and snapping your picture as you laze around in your old clothes ?

At over 100,000, the population of Nogales, Sonora dwarfs that of Nogales, Arizona at 17,000. Some Americans are shocked by Nogales, Sonora if they have never seen a border town before. There are kids in rags everywhere and some of the buildings seem ready to fall over.

But, as you start to deal with the people in the stores you find them warm-hearted and fun. Take the time to chat and bargain. Most prices, except for the more formal stores, are very negotiable and you are expected to bargain. Still, there is no prize for squeezing the last nickel of a little deal, try to be fair to the vendors.

There is a bewildering variety of inexpensive crafts available. Look around for a while before you buy, many of the articles are the same and the prices vary wildly from shop to shop.

Maybe the best bargains are the rugs made by the **Zapotec Indians** in Mexico. Many are Navajo or Hopi patterns done very well at a fraction of the price of the real thing. Pottery, blankets, leather goods and other crafts are also excellent bargains. In the shops on the east side of the railroad tracks are several **better jewelry shops** and a very **interesting antique shop** on the first floor of the building with the **La Roca** restaurant. In contrast, street vendors hawk "gold" "Rolex" watches for $25 dollars and a lot of similar junk.

The food in Nogales can be excellent but be real careful about sampling street vendors food. Favorite fancy eateries are **La Roca** , **El Cid** and **El Greco.** The seafood and traditional Mexican food is worth the drive to Nogales even if you don't care about the shopping. All serve the excellent **Guaymas shrimp**, a treat. **Elviras** next to the fence about two blocks west of the gate serves traditional Sonoran food in an informal setting and throws in a free shot of tequila.

1. Old Santa Cruz Country Courthouse
2. Pimeria Alta Historical Society Museum
3. Federal Building and Parking

EMPIRE-CIENEGA RESOURCE CONSERVATION AREA

Area of Town: 45 miles southeast.

Map Reference: X7.

Phone Number: 602-629-5321 (U.S. Bureau of Land Management).

Directions: Take I-10 east to exit 281 and go south for 18 miles on Hwy 83, then go left at the sign for the RCA.

Best Time of Year: All year.

Best Time of Day: Early and late for the best light and to see wildlife; avoid midday from the end of May till the end of September.

Hours: 24 hours.

Rules: No off road driving.

Fees: None.

Facilities: No water or facilities but picnicking and primitive camping are allowed.

Nearby Places of Interest: Sonoita; Patagonia.

Comments:

D riving through the grasslands gives you a chance to look it over carefully without having to do a lot of hiking. There is a kiosk about a half mile from the highway with a map and the only interpretive material you will see. Plenty of wildflowers provide color in season and there seems to be something blooming almost the whole year. In June the soap tree yuccas with their huge displays of creamy white blossoms are especially striking.

The road runs for 10 miles or so northeast past the ranch headquarters to the creek with many **big cottonwoods**. If it has been raining, the ford just past the ranch may be too high to cross but the bottom is firm if the water is shallow. There is a big meadow at the end of the road with some decent camp sites on the north end.

The RCA is composed of grasslands, oak woodland, marshes called **cienegas** [Spanish for hundred waters] and a stream with flowing water. The water provides habitat for wildlife including deer, **pronghorn antelope**, javelina and over 160 species of birds. Huge old cottonwoods line the creek, as well as groves of mesquite and desert willow.

Take a hike along the creek to get a look at the abundant birdlife. In November or December the cottonwoods will turn golden and the light can be very nice. Also, the big meadow with the backdrop of the Whetstone Mountains to the east is picturesque especially when the tall grass has dried to a beautiful wheat color.

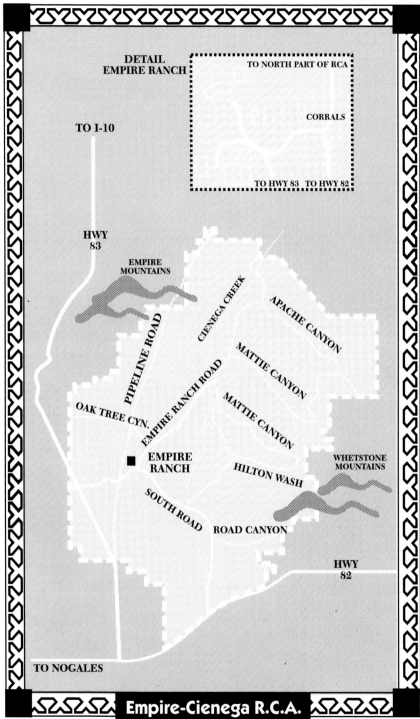

DETAIL
EMPIRE RANCH

TO NORTH PART OF RCA

CORRALS

TO I-10

TO HWY 83   TO HWY 82

HWY
83

EMPIRE
MOUNTAINS

CIENEGA CREEK

APACHE CANYON

PIPELINE ROAD

MATTIE CANYON

EMPIRE RANCH ROAD

MATTIE CANYON

OAK TREE CYN.

EMPIRE
RANCH

HILTON WASH

WHETSTONE
MOUNTAINS

SOUTH ROAD

ROAD CANYON

HWY
82

TO NOGALES

Empire-Cienega R.C.A.

KARTCHNER CAVERNS STATE PARK

Area of Town: 35 miles southeast.
Map Reference: X7.
Phone Number: 602-542-4174 (Arizona State Parks Dept. Phoenix).
Directions: 16 miles south of Benson on Hwy. 90.
Nearby Places of Interest: San Pedro Riparian Nat'l Conservation Area, Fort Huachuca.

Comments:

This spectacular cave was discovered by cavers almost twenty years ago and was kept secret for over 15 years while arrangements were made with the state to acquire and protect it. It became a state park in 1988 but extraordinary measures are being taken to protect the natural environment of this "living" cave before it is opened to the public, in 1994 or 1995.

Some of the most phenomenal cave formations ever found exist here. There is a soda straw formation 1/4 inch in diameter and 20 feet long.

Check with the Arizona State Parks Board to make sure it is open before your visit.

Hedgehog cactus.

ꮺꮴꭲ꭛ꮴꭲꮿꮴꭲꭘꮴꭲꭘꮴꭲꭘꮴꭲ SONOITA

Area of Town: 40 miles southeast.

Map Reference: X6.

Directions: Take I-10 east to exit 281 and go south for about 20 miles on Hwy 83.

Best Time of Year: All year.

Best Time of Day: Early and late for the best light but it is pretty anytime.

Hours: 24 hours.

Rules: Be very careful with cigarettes because of the fire danger.

Fees: None.

Facilities: National Forest picnic facilities along Hwy 83; shops and restaurants in Sonoita

Nearby Places of Interest: Patagonia, San Pedro Riparian National Conservation Area.

Comments:

The attraction of this trip is the scenery as the highway winds through beautiful rolling grasslands studded with oak trees. Nearer Sonoita the land flattens out into plains which look like the midwest, indeed the

movie "Giant" was filmed here. This has been cattle country since the 1690's when Father Kino introduced 150 head of cattle.

There are a few stores and restaurants, including a good steak house, at the junction of Hwy 82. From the junction you can head out to many adventures. Here are a few suggested options:

Option #1. Eat, get back in the car and return to Tucson. A nice easy trip.

Option #2. Drive back north on Highway 83 a few miles and hike in the **Empire-Cienega Resource Area** (see previous section). You can stretch your legs without committing to a hard hike. There are no trails per se but there is plenty of open country to wander around.

Option #3. Continue south on Hwy 82 for 12 miles to **Patagonia**, tour there and then return via Sonoita. Still an easy trip, plus there is a really good restaurant in Patagonia and you can see the bird sanctuary.

Option #4. Continue south on Hwy 82, see Patagonia then continue south on Hwy 82 to Nogales and return to Tucson on I-19. Very scenic but a little long, allow several hours for driving as the roads are winding.

Option #5. Go east on Hwy 82 to Hwy 90 then turn north and drive back to Tucson. This is a manageable drive with fine scenery, especially **Rain Valley**, just before you drop down the hill to highway 90.

Option #7. Go back north on Hwy 83 about 7 miles and turn left on Greaterville Rd. This road turns to dirt and winds many miles over the north end of the Santa Rita Mountains, coming out near Madera Canyon on Continental Rd. which takes you to I-19 and back to town. The road is rough but usually passable to passenger cars.

PATAGONIA

Area of Town: Southeast 60 miles.

Map Reference: Y 5.

Phone Number: 602-394-2400.(Nature Conservancy).

Directions: Take I-10 east to exit 281, then go south for 24 miles on Hwy 83 to Hwy 82, make a right and go another 12 miles.

Best Time of Year: Anytime, but if it has been storming there is a strong chance you will not be able to cross the creek to get to the bird sanctuary. March through September are the best for birding.

Best Time of Day: The elevation here is about 4,000 feet so it is a little cooler than Tucson. Early and late are best for the light. It will be nice all day in the trees along the creek except for midday in the summer.

Hours: 24 hours, except the Patagonia Sonoita Creek Preserve is closed Monday and Tuesday and is open 7:30 am to 3:30 pm Wednesday to Sunday.

Rules: Lots of rules in the Patagonia Sonita Creek Preserve, including no picnicking, bicycling, camping, fires or pets.

Fees: $3.00 donation for the Preserve.

Facilities: Picnicking and restrooms in the Patagonia Town Park; restaurants and a few shops and galleries.

Nearby Places of Interest: Sonoit; Nogales.

Comments:

This pretty little town is set in a wooded creek bottom. Originally a railhead for the mining towns to the east, today Patagonia sleeps in its memories. Its low key charm has drawn many artists who display their work in several small galleries. Among the restaurants a favorite is "The Ovens" a gourmet deli and bakery run by a couple who are so fit you can't believe they ever eat any of their own cheesecake.

Patagonia Sonoita Creek Preserve operated by the **Nature Conservancy** is an extraordinary desert environment. The running creek is crowded with enormous 130-year old Fremont cottonwoods, Arizona walnuts and numerous rare and endangered plant species. Birdwatchers from all over the world flock here to see over 260 bird species including several like the gray hawk and green kingfisher rarely seen elsewhere.

To get to the Preserve turn on 3rd St. at the Patagonia Market and make a left on Pennsylvania and follow that across the creek and on to the Preserve on the left. Hours and fees are listed above. Guided tours are offered on Saturday at 9:00 am and other tours are seasonal; call 602-394-2400 for a current schedule.

Patagonia Lake State Park (602-287-6965) just south of town offers fishing, boating, picnicking and camping. Sonoita Creek Trail is a 1.2 mile round trip which leaves from the east end of the east camp ground. There are petroglyphs on the opposite side of the lake.

East of town are the **ghost towns of Washington Camp, Duquesne** and **Harshaw** in the Patagonia Mountains. This is a rugged area and directions are difficult to follow among the many old mining roads. I would suggest getting one of the books on ghost towns available for this area. At least have the Coronado National Forest Map for the Nogales and Sierra Vista Districts. Remember, there are open vertical mine shafts. Many are like ant traps, they look easy to approach but the sides are sloped and slippery. Once you start moving you'll end up in the bottom, maybe a long way down. Horizontal shafts present their own dangers with rotten timbers and maybe a rattlesnake getting out of the hot sun.

You might be tempted to drive the dirt roads east from Patagonia to Parker Canyon Lake or Bisbee. It can be done and the roads are not all that bad but it is **slow going** and will take several hours even though the distance is not great. There are no services between Patagonia and Bisbee. Once in Bisbee it is still a two hour drive back to Tucson. If you do brave it you will see some of the most beautiful and remote country in southern Arizona.

Montezuma Pass at the south end of the **Huachuca Mountains** is in the **Coronado National Monument** and provides a panoramic view of the country covered by **Francisco Vásquez de Coronado** and his men in 1540-1541 on an expedition that eventually led them as far north as Wichita, Kansas in a vain search for **Cíbola**, the legendary **City of Gold**. If you get this far you will also feel like you have been on a long expedition after grinding along for hours on the back roads from Patagonia. An easier way to see Montezuma Pass is from Sierra Vista where the dirt road part will only be a few miles.

Another loop drive back to Tucson that is not as demanding is to continue south on Hwy 82 for 20 miles to **Nogales** and then come back on I-19.

San Pedro River, ©Randy Prentice

SAN PEDRO RIPARIAN NATIONAL CONSERVATION AREA

Area of Town: 60 miles southeast.

Map Reference: W-48.

Phone Number: 602-457-2265 (BLM Conservation Area Office).

Directions: I-10 east to exit 303 or 304 at Benson then south through St. David on Hwy 80 to Hwy 82 and turn right and continue west for 6 miles to the BLM office at Fairbanks. This is a very big area and more specific directions to other parts are contained in the comments section below.

Best Time of Year: All year but it will be too hot to hike midday in the summer.

Best Time of Day: Early and late for the wildlife and the best light; if it is cold in the winter it may be well to wait for the sun to warm things up a bit.

Hours: 24 hours; you can get the permits required for backcountry areas at self serve stations at all visitor parking areas.

Rules: Lots, including pets on leash in developed areas and posted areas, mountain bikes or cars on designated roads only, no mining or removing artifacts including tin cans and glass bottles, no metal detectors.

Fees: $1.50 per person for backcountry camping.

Facilities: Restrooms at BLM headquarters; no water available in Conservation Area.

Nearby Places of Interest: Tombstone; Bisbee.

Comments:

The SPRNCA consists of a narrow strip of land 35 miles long flanking the **San Pedro River** from the Mexican border to **St. David**.The BLM office at Fairbanks has a wealth of free printed handouts about the area, its flora and fauna and human history.

Good hiking can be found starting from the **San Pedro House** just west of the river on Highway 90. The San Pedro house contains a natural history bookstore run by the **Friends of the San Pedro River**. The access at **Hereford Road** also is a fine hiking area with huge cottonwood trees ranging up and down the valley. A two-mile round trip hike north from the **Charleston Road** crossing will lead to the ghost towns of **Charleston** and **Milltown** which processed the silver ore from Tombstone in the 1880's.

The star attraction of the SPRNCA is the bird life with over 350 species to be seen. There are 35 species of raptors alone to be found in addition to exotic species like the **green kingfisher** and **yellow-billed cuckoo**.

The San Pedro had been inhabited for 12,000 years and mammoth kills with Clovis spear points have been excavated near the Hereford Crossing.

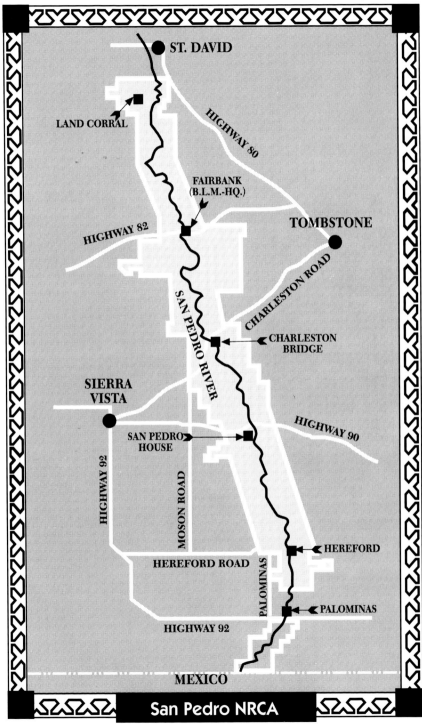

ST. DAVID

LAND CORRAL

HIGHWAY 80

FAIRBANK
(B.L.M.-HQ.)

HIGHWAY 82

TOMBSTONE

SAN PEDRO RIVER

CHARLESTON ROAD

CHARLESTON
BRIDGE

SIERRA
VISTA

SAN PEDRO
HOUSE

HIGHWAY 90

HIGHWAY 92

MOSON ROAD

HEREFORD

HEREFORD ROAD

PALOMINAS

PALOMINAS

HIGHWAY 92

MEXICO

San Pedro NRCA

Mr. Ed Lehner found the first evidence on his ranch in the early 1950's when he saw mammoth bones protruding from the banks of a wash. The site was excavated and stone tools and weapons were discovered with the bones. Mr. Lehner maintains a museum in his home and will give you a tour of the site by appointment. (602-366-5554).

In 1540 **Francisco Vásquez de Coronado** and his men passed through the San Pedro River Valley on an expedition that eventually led them as far north as Wichita, Kansas in a vain search for Cíbola, the legendary City of Gold. There is no physical evidence of his passing.

In the late 1690's Father Kino introduced cattle to Sonoita to the west. By 1775 there was enough Spanish activity in the area that **Presidio Santa Cruz de Terrenate** was established to protect the missionaries and colonists. It only lasted about five years, a victim of constant Apache attacks in which 80 persons were killed. The site is preserved and may be visited. Go west on Hwy 82 about 1.5 miles from the BLM office at Fairbanks to Kellar Rd., then turn north for about two miles and you will see a pullout on the right with an access through the fence. There is a marked trail from there for 1.2 miles to the Presidio site where there is a self-guided tour.

AMERIND FOUNDATION

Area of Town: 65 miles east.
Map Reference: W8.
Phone Number: 602-586-3666.
Directions: Take I-10 east to exit 318 and turn right on the blacktop road. The foundation is about 0.5 miles on the left; it is well signed.
Best Time of Year: All year.
Hours: 10:00 am to 4:00 pm; closed major holidays.
Fees: Adults $3.00; seniors & children 12 to 18 $2.00; under 12 free.
Facilities: Museum; art gallery; museum shop; picnic area.
Nearby Places of Interest: Cochise Stronghold.

Comments:

William Shirley Fulton established the Amerind [American Indian] Foundation to preserve Native American artifacts he had collected in the southwest. This is a fine private museum of Native American artifacts and interpretive material. The art gallery housing the family art collection has some fine western works. The grounds and surrounding country are covered with huge granite boulders and oak trees, creating a compelling scene.

Facing Page: Climbers in Cochise Stronghold

Day Trips

COCHISE STRONGHOLD

Area of Town: 70 miles southeast.

Map Reference: W8.

Phone Number: 602-670-6483 (Coronado National Forest).

Directions: I-10 east from Tucson to the Dragoon exit # 318. Go through Dragoon and head east about 7.5 miles from the post office to Stronghold Rd. and make a right. Follow Stronghold Rd. 6 miles to its end and make a right and follow the road into the Stronghold. If you get lost you can also go in from 666 south of Willcox.

Best Time of Year: Each part of the year has its charm but it will be very hot in the summer.

Best Time of Day: Depends on the time of year. In warmer weather the cool morning will be nice but in the winter it may be too chilly. The light is best early and late.

Hours: 24 hours.

Rules: Be very careful with fire.

Fees: None, except for the campground.

Facilities: Picnic and camping facilities; restrooms.

Nearby Places of Interest: Amerind Foundation; ghosttown of Pearce; Fort Huachuca.

Comments:

The Apaches made these mountains famous when they used the rugged canyons as a stronghold for their raids on other tribes, the Mexicans and Americans. The canyons are extremely rugged and difficult to navigate. Legend has it that Cochise was buried along with his horse by being lowered into a large crack in the cliffs.

A hiking trail ascends from the campground through the oak forest and granite boulders to the crest of the range and leads down the other side to the West Stronghold. It is a pleasant walk, just remember to take plenty of water. Allow 2 hours round-trip

Another good hike starts from the boulder in the middle of the road just before the campground. This is the way rock climbers get to Rockfellow and Cochise Domes, among others. Follow the vague route up the drainage; it branches many times, best to keep to the left. If you are lucky enough to follow the route to the top of the valley (takes about an hour) you will end up wandering among a fairyland of huge boulders. It is easy to get lost doing this hike, if you are not up to some adventure and routefinding stick with the maintained trail from the campground.

ᛁᚵᛁᚦᛁᛁᚵᛁᚦᛁᛁᚵᛁᚦᛁᛁᚵᛁᚦᛁᛁᚵ FORT HUACHUCA

Area of Town: 65 miles southeast.

Map Reference: Y7.

Phone Number: 602-533-5736 (Fort Huachuca Museum).

Directions: I-10 east to Hwy 90 (exit 302), then south to Sierra Vista, do not take the Hwy 90 bypass of Sierra Vista, go straight to Fry Blvd. and make a right and you will be right at the main gate for the Army Post.

Best Time of Year: All year.

Best Time of Day: Anytime, but Sierra Vista is at over 4600 feet, so it will be cooler in the winter. It may be more comfortable to wait until the sun warms things up a bit at this time of year.

Hours: 9:00 am to 4:00 pm Monday through Friday; 1:00 pm to 4:00 pm weekends.

Rules: Pick up a visitor's pass at the gate to the post.

Fees: None.

Facilities: Gift shop; restrooms.

Nearby Places of Interest: Amerind Foundation; San Pedro Riparian Conservation Area; Tombstone; Coronado National Monument; Ramsey Canyon.

Comments:

Fort Huachuca was founded in **1877** to serve as a base for troops fighting the **Apaches**. Driving through the grasslands around Fort Huachuca imagine yourself as a nineteen-year-old trooper riding horseback through the tall grass looking for Apaches. The Apaches were legendary among the troops for their ability to disappear in the terrain. Seldom fighting fixed battles, they preferred stealth. Constant watchfulness was the price of life when they were about. A casual trooper easily became a dead trooper in Apache country.

Like many military posts, Fort Huachuca has grown a fringe of intense commercial development but the areas surrounding the city are of outstanding natural beauty. The Fort has been a base for **tank training** for many years and you can seen the evidence of that on the ridges of the **Huachuca Mountains** beyond the post. The principal mission of the post today is the sophisticated radio communication which forms the nerve system of the modern battle field. Many troops from the Fort served with distinction in the recent Desert Shield and Desert Storm operations. Incidentally, the big balloon you may see above the Fort is operated as a radar surveillance device to detect drug smuggling planes coming in from Mexico.

The **Fort Huachuca Museum** is a fine facility with full coverage in

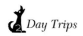

photos and interpretive material tracing the Fort from its Indian fighting days to the present. The contribution of the **"Buffalo Soldiers,"** black troopers, are remembered in special exhibitions.

A trip to Fort Huachuca can be easily combined with a visit to **Ramsey Canyon Preserve** (covered in the next section) and **Coronado National Memorial**.

To get to the Coronado National Memorial take Hwy 92 south from Sierra Vista about 12 miles to a well-signed turnoff. The dirt road is OK for passenger cars but if you opt for the drive all the way to the top of Montezuma Pass it will be kind of bumpy.

The Memorial commemorates the passing of the Spanish expeditionary force led by **Francisco Vásquez de Coronado** in **1540**. They were looking for the legendary seven cities of gold, **Cíbola**. Eventually they ended up near **Wichita, Kansas** but never found the gold. This trip was typical of Spanish exploration in the new world, both in its tenacity and boldness and in the willingness of the Spanish to believe the Indians they questioned. The Indians, whether in Florida, Alabama, New Mexico or Arizona always told the Spanish the gold they sought was far to the north. In hindsight it is plain the Indians were simply trying to get the Spanish to keep moving out of their neighborhood.

Hummingbirds at feeder.

RAMSEY CANYON

Area of Town: 80 miles southeast.

Map Reference: Y7.

Phone Number: 602-378-2785 (Nature Conservancy).

Directions: I-10 east to exit 302, then south on Hwy 90 and then Hwy 92 past Sierra Vista (or stop at the Fort Huachuca Museum), right on Ramsey Canyon Rd. about 6 miles south of the Sierra Vista city limits.

Best Time of Year: All year, but it will be pretty cool in winter.

Hours: 8:00 am to 5:00 pm.

Rules: Permit must be obtained at book store before walking the trails; no picnicking or camping; no buses, trailers or RV's over 20 feet; smoking in the parking area only; no pets; no radios or tape players; no bicycles; do not feed the critters; and don't play with that thing, you are going to put out someone's eye.

Fees: A $3.00 donation is suggested for non-members.

Facilities: Restrooms; book shop; cabins.

Nearby Places of Interest: Fort Huachuca; Coronado National Monument.

Comments:

The appeal of this lovely spot is the total quiet and peace that prevails. The Nature Conservancy which operates the preserve has accomplished this atmosphere by making the hard choice that public agencies can seldom make: they strictly limit the number of visitors. This is accomplished by the simple expedient of having a very small parking lot and not permitting parking anywhere else. Reservations are recommended, although you might get lucky and find room if you just show up.

The Preserve is famous the world over to birders and the cabins are usually full of visitors who have planned a trip to catch a special bird event like the hummingbird migration in August.

Among the wildlife which are seen in the preserve are coatimundi, deer, javelina and black bear. Birds are legion and include, in season, golden eagles, 12 species of hummingbirds, whiskered screech owls and goshawks.

The hiking in the canyon varies from the casual 0.7-mile walk around Ramsey Creek to the steeper Hamburg trail which heads uphill into the Coronado National Forest. There are excellent overviews of the spectacular canyon from the Hamburg Trail.

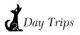

TOMBSTONE

Area of Town: 70 miles southeast.

Map Reference: X8.

Phone Number: 602-457-3929 (Tombstone Visitors Center);602-457-3311 (Tombstone Courthouse State Historical Park).

Directions: I-10 east to exit 303 or 304 at Benson then south through St. David on Hwy 80 to Tombstone.

Best Time of Year: All year; Helldorado Days are one weekend in mid-October.

Best Time of Day: The attractions are only going to be open during regular business hours; avoid midday in the summer.

Hours: They vary. The State Historical Park in the old courthouse is open from 8:00 am to 5:00 pm. The OK Corral from 8:30 am to 5:00 pm. The Historama from 9:00 am to 4:00 pm. On Sunday at 2:00 pm there are reenactments of brawls and famous shoot-outs either in the street on Allen St. or at the OK Corral. Check with the visitors center about special events.

Rules: None partner, this is the town too tough to die.

Fees: State Park is $2.00 for adults over 18; $1.00 age 12-17. Others attractions vary.

Facilities: The City Park has restrooms and picnic tables.

Nearby Places of Interest: Bisbee, San Pedro Riparian National Conservation Area.

Comments:

Tombstone is "The town too tough to die," although it might be a little embarrassed by the hoopla that keeps its old image alive. There are many "roadside attractions" here such as the world's largest rose bush, Boothill and a **"Historama"** with the late **Vincent Price** narrating the showdown at the OK corral and other historic Tombstone events

Tombstone was founded in **1879** after a silver strike by a prospector from nearby **Fort Huachuca**, who ignored the advice of the calvarymen that the only thing he would find was his tombstone. They assumed the Apaches would kill him but he was very lucky and found silver ore on the surface. **Edward Schieffelin** sold out for $300,000—a very big fortune in those days and lived to prospect all over the west and Alaska.

The town reached a **population of 15,000** by the **mid-1880's** but went bust when the mines hit the water table at 1500 feet and were unable to continue. Today there are mining operations in the prospects but not on the old scale.

The Cochise County seat was located here before the mines failed and was housed in what was called the **"Million Dollar Courthouse."** Today it is a State Historical Park and contains interpretive exhibits with numerous interesting photos from the 1800's.

There are many picturesque buildings here besides the Million Dollar Courthouse. Also, boot hill is fascinating, particularly the epitaphs of those who died violent deaths. The number of Chinese buried there also gives an indication of their contribution to the building of the west.

Bisbee is located 24 miles south and actually has more to see, including the huge "Lavender Pit" open pit copper mine and the rambling town covering the precipitous hillsides with miners houses, many still occupied.

To the east of Tombstone about 13 miles on a good dirt road is the **ghost town of Gleeson.** It was established in **1900** on the site of an older mining camp called **Turquoise** which had been the location of mining for turquoise by the Indians. The bar might be open but nothing else survives since mining was discontinued in **1939**. There are many old buildings and mining works and colorful tailings piles can be seen on the mountainsides. If you continue on the dirt road it swings north past more old mines to the ghost town of **Pearce** and then hooks up with Hwy 666 which takes you back to I-10, a pretty manageable loop drive.

Boot hill

BISBEE

Area of Town: 96 miles southeast.

Map Reference: Y8.

Phone Number: 602-432-7071 (Mining & Historical Museum); 602-432-2071 (Copper Queen Mine Tour); 602-432-2216 (Copper Queen Hotel).

Directions: I-10 east to Benson, take exit 303 go through town and head south on Hwy 80, go through St. David and Tombstone and you can't miss it.

Best Time of Year: All year; it is especially appealing in the summer because at 5,300 feet it will be a lot cooler than Tucson.

Best Time of Day: There are great photo opportunities here which means you might want to plan to be here early or late for the good light.

Hours: The shops restaurants and galleries keep usual business hours; the hours of some of the attractions are listed in the comments section.

Rules: Pets on leash.

Fees: None, except for the attractions like the tours.

Facilities: Shops, galleries, restaurants; restrooms in the post office.

Nearby Places of Interest: Tombstone; Douglas.

Comments:

Located at 5,300 feet in the **Mule Mountains**, Bisbee is a visual delight. The buildings, from grand hotel to miners' shacks, stagger up and down the steep sides of the canyons. Old clapboard houses with tiny little gardens perch at the top of tortuous staircases a hundred feet or more up from the street level. They are occupied by an eclectic variety of folks drawn to the casual atmosphere and the excellent climate.

Bisbee is compact enough to enjoy the tour outlined in the Chamber of Commerce Bisbee Walking Tour. There are many craft and jewelry shops as well as galleries and restaurants. The **Copper Queen Hotel** is the pride of Bisbee and has a decent restaurant but there are several other excellent eatiers nearby.

The first mining activity at Bisbee was in the mid **1870's** and a major copper deposit was discovered. It was mined extensively until **1974** when the great Lavender Pit was closed. Underground mining ceased the next year.

The mine drew workers from the world over and much of the color of Bisbee's early days came from the unionizing efforts and political leaning of the work force. During a strike in **1917** the local business community, convinced it was saving itself from a communist menace, decided to take matters in its own hands. Pinkertons and other thugs were deputized to roust **1,000 striking miners** from their homes one night. They were

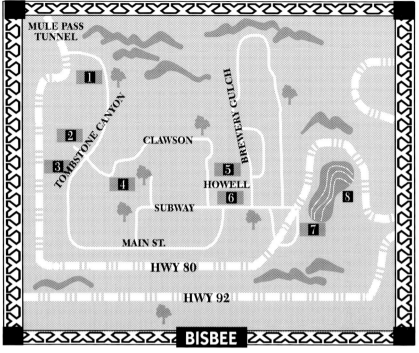

1. School House Inn
2. Historic Courthouse
3. Inn At Castle Rock
4. The Clawson House
5. Copper Queen Hotel
6. Mining Museum
7. Copper Queen Mine Tour
8. Lavender Pit

loaded at gun point into railroad boxcars supplied by the Phelps Dodge Company and dumped in the New Mexico desert. The U.S. Army rescued the miners and set up a tent city. The miners never returned to Bisbee.

The deportation of the miners and the rest of Bisbee's history is superbly presented at the **Mining and Historical Museum** located just across from the Copper Queen Hotel. This is one of the finest local history museums you will ever see, the history comes alive in the professionally done exhibits.

While wandering around town do not fail to visit the **Cochise County Courthouse** on Tombstone Canyon. Still active as the county court house, it is a real beauty. The interior has extensive brass fittings and the broad stairways and grand appointments bespeak a bygone era.

A mile south of downtown is **Lavender Pit**, a huge open pit copper mine which allowed low grade ore to be economically recovered. A tour of the pit is available from the Queen Mine Building daily at noon. See below for details.

The perils of more traditional underground mining can be experi-

enced by taking the Copper Queen Mine Tour. This is a great experience. You will ride a mine car into the bowels of the earth and learn how the copper was blasted out of the tunnels by miners drilling by hand and using candles for light. Not for the claustrophobic. Bring a sweater, it is cold. If you forget, they have an interesting collection of jackets to lend you. Narrated by real miners, the tour takes 60 to 75 minutes and starts daily at 10:30 am, noon, 2:00 pm and 3:30 pm. Fees: adults $8.00; children 7-11 $3.50; children 3-6 $1.75. Reservations are recommended, 602-432-2071. Tickets are purchased at the Queen Mine Building adjacent to downtown, across Hwy 80.

Lodgings

Many people like to stay over night in Bisbee to soak up the atmosphere, see **La Vuelta de Bisbee** (bicycle race) or whatever. There are no big chain motels here so the following list of lodgings is provided so you can call to make reservations. They are listed alphabetically, in case you didn't notice.

1. **Bisbee Grand Hotel**, 61 Main St., Old Bisbee (602-432-5900). A fine B&B/Small Hotel. Located right downtown.
2. **Clawson House B&B**, 116C Clawson Ave., Old Bisbee (602-432-5237). A very elegantly decorated house with three rooms only. Sometimes closed while the owners go fishing in January, you will probably need reservations anytime.
3. **Copper Queen Hotel**, 11 Howell St., Old Bisbee (602-432-2216). At the center of Bisbee and a standard for many visitors. This comes closest to a regular hotel in Bisbee.
4. **Gadsden Hotel**, 1046 G Ave, Douglas (602-364-4481). Located 12 miles east in Douglas it is the most grand of all the hotels listed here. Five stories with a huge lobby and enormous Tiffany stained glass windows. It is often the hub of local social activities. Highly recommended.
5. **Inn at Castle Rock**, 112 Tombstone Canyon Rd., Old Bisbee (602-432-4449 or 432-719). A charming old favorite, a little worn but with a very comfortable feel.
6. **Jonquil Motel**, 317 Tombstone Canyon, Old Bisbee (602-432-7371). Very small, unpretentious facility several blocks from downtown.
7. **Main Street Inn**, 26 Main St., Old Bisbee (602-432-5237). Very nice B&B run by the owners of the Clawson House.
8. **OK Jailhouse Inn**, 9 OK St., Old Bisbee (602-432-7435). Only one fancy suite, it is truly unique. The bars on the doors and windows are

Facing Page: Copper Queen Mine Tour

reminders of the building's original purpose.

9. **Oliver House**, 24 Sowle, Old Bisbee (602-432-4286). A restored executive inn for a mining company, it provides easy access to down town.

10. **Park Place B&B**, 200 East Vista, Warren (602-432-3054). Good views of the park, in a fine restored home.

11. **San Jose Lodge & RV Park**, 1002 Naco Highway, San Jose (602-432-5761).

12. **School House Inn**, 818 Tombstone Canyon, Old Bisbee (800-537-4333; 602-432-2996). This converted 1918 school house is the cream of the crop of bed and breakfast places in Bisbee. Private baths, big beautiful rooms, terraces and patio dining. You will like it!

13. **The White House B&B**, 800 Congdon Ave., Warren (602-432-7215). Located just down the road from Bisbee it is worth the trip. Jetted tubs, heated towels, linen and lace. Obviously they are out to pamper you.

14. **Turquoise Valley Golf & RV Park**, Newell Rd. off Naco Highway (602-432-3091).

CHIRICAHUA NATIONAL MONUMENT

Area of Town: 120 miles east.

Map Reference: W 10.

Phone Number: 602-824-3560 (National Monument Headquarters).

Directions: I-10 east to Willcox exit # 340, south through Willcox on Hwy 186, then east to the Monument. Willcox is the last chance to get gas or food.

Best Time of Year: All year.

Best Time of Day: All day but it can be very cool on winter mornings as the elevation is 6,870 feet at Massai Point.

Hours: 24 hours.

Rules: Pets on leash and they are not permitted on the best trails.

Fees: $4.00 per car entrance fee; $6.00 for camping.

Facilities: Attended Visitors Center sells books & maps; picnic areas; camping, including RV sites.

Nearby Places of Interest: On the way down Hwy 186 you will pass the turn off for Fort Bowie National Historical Site. It is a dirt road drive but well worth doing to see Apache Pass and the fort established to control it. There is an attended visitors center at Ft. Bowie with interpretive material.

Comments:

Chiricahua National Monument is about a two hour drive from Tucson. You will pass through some of the most beautiful and remote cattle country in Arizona. The views are worth the trip.

The monument itself was established to showcase a fantastic garden of giant rhyolite spires. Balanced rocks, strange figures and outrageous colors combine with complete silence to give an awesome feel to this place. The hikes are moderate and wind among formations with names like Duck on a Rock, the Totem Pole and Big Balanced Rock. A favorite hike is from Massai Point down through the Heart of Rocks and then down the creek, passing through the forest back to the visitors center.

It is estimated that fewer than 5% of the Monument's visitors use the trail system. This is due in part to the fact that many arrive in summer when temperatures tend to be high. In all but the heat of the summer, though, the trails can easily be enjoyed. The elevation of the monument, 5,400 feet at the visitors center and 6,870 at Massai Point, makes for cooler temperatures. Even if you elect not to hike, the views from the road pullouts and from Massai Point are worth the drive.

ᛝᚢᚱᛖᛒᚢ CALENDAR OF EVENTS ᚢᚱᛖᛒᚢᚱ

Current dates for these events will be listed in the Tucson Official Visitors Guide available at the Metropolitan Tucson Convention & Visitors Bureau, 130 S. Scott Ave, Tucson, Az. 85701, 602-624-1817, Fax 602-884-7804.

JANUARY

Casino Gambling
Las Vegas-style gambling hall on the Tohono O'odham reservation.
7350 S. Old Nogales Hwy
889-7354

Motorcycle Ice Racing
Tucson Convention Center
791-4266

Professional Tennis Tournament
Randolph Park Tennis Center
791-4896

Professional Golf Association Tournament
Tucson National & Starr Pass Golf Courses
624-4653

Rillito Downs Quarter Horse Racing
Parimutuel betting and a colorful atmosphere. (see p. 135)
N.1st Ave. & Rillito River
740-2690

Southern Arizona Square, Round Dance & Clogging Festival
Tucson Convention Center
791-4266

Tucson Quilters Guild Show
Tucson Convention Center
791-4266

University of Arizona Basketball
McKale Center
621-2411

FEBRUARY

Casino Gambling
Las Vegas-style gambling hall on the Tohono O'odham reservation.
7350 S. Old Nogales Hwy
889-7354

Fiddler's Contest
Reid Park
791-4079

Greyhound Racing
Tucson Greyhound Park
2601 S. 3rd. Ave
884-7576

Indian Arts Show & Benefit
Old Town Artisans
623-6024

La Reunion del Fuerte
Fort Lowell neighborhood history walk.
Fort Lowell Park
327-4286

La Fiesta de los Vaqueros (see p. 133)
Professional Rodeo
Tucson Rodeo Grounds
741-2233 (Tickets)

Old Pueblo Balloon Classic
Midvale Park (see p. 142)
883-7504

Rillito Downs Quarter Horse Racing
Parimutuel betting and a colorful atmosphere.(see p. 135)
N.1st Ave. & Rillito River
740-2690

Tubac Festival of the Arts
Tubac (see p. 162)
602-398-2704

Tucson Gem & Mineral Show
Tucson Convention Center
791-4266 (Convention Center)
322-5773 (Tucson Gem & Mineral Society)

Tucson Marathon
26 miles through the city
326-9383

Tucson Rodeo Parade
741-2233 (see p. 134)

University of Arizona Baseball
Sancet Field
621-2411

University of Arizona Basketball
McKale Center
621-2411

World of Wheels Car Show
Tucson Convention Center
791-4266

MARCH

Aerospace & Arizona Day (Sometimes in April)
Spectacular airshow over Davis Monthan Airbase,featuring the Air Force Blue Angels

Facing Page: Heart of Rocks and Cochise Head, Chiricahua Monument,
©*Edward McCain*   195

 *Calendar of Events*

Davis-Monthan Airbase
750-3204

Arts & Crafts Fair
Fort Lowell Park
791-4063

Casino Gambling
Las Vegas-style gambling hall
on the Tohono O'odham
reservation.
7350 S. Old Nogales Hwy
889-7354

Colorado Rockies Spring Training
Hi Corbett Field, Reid Park
791-4266

Greyhound Racing
Tucson Greyhound Park
2601 S. 3rd. Ave
884-7576

Ladies Pro Golf Association Tournament
Randolf Park Golf Course
791-4896

Rillito Downs Horse Racing (see p. 135)
*Parimutuel betting and a
colorful atmosphere.*
N.1st Ave. & Rillito River
740-2690

Ski Carnival
Mount Lemmon Ski Valley
576-1321

Spring Plant Sale
Tucson Botanical Gardens
326-9255

Territorial Days
*Town birthday celebration,
firecart races.*
Tombstone
602-457-2211

Tucson Festival
*Celebrates Tucson's Native
American, Hispanic &
Territorial cultural history*
Himmel Park
622-6911

University of Arizona Baseball
Sancet Field
621-2411

University of Arizona Basketball
McKale Center
621-2411

Wa:k Pow Wow
*Tohono O'odhan Tribe;
Intertribal dancing, fiddlers'
contest.*
Mission San Xavier del Bac
294-5727

APRIL

4th Avenue Street Fair (see p. 147)
Huge selection of arts & crafts,
food & street entertainers.
4th Avenue at University
624-5004

Casino Gambling
Las Vegas-style gambling hall on
the Tohono O'odham
reservation.
7350 S. Old Nogales Hwy
889-7354

Celebrity Tennis Classic
Randolph Tennis Center,
Reid Park
795-9949

Concerto K-tal
*Traditional and popular Mexican
music.*
Reid Park
791-4079

Greyhound Racing
Tucson Greyhound Park
2601 S. 3rd. Ave
884-7576

Gun Show
Pima County Fairgrounds
762-5867

Home Garden Tour
Tucson Botanical Gardens
326-9255

La Vuelta de Bisbee
*Thrilling week-long bicycle race
draws top racers from all over
the country.*
Bisbee
602-432-5421

Pima County Fair
*Traditional County Fair with
4-H competition, carnival, horse
shows and big name
entertainment.*
Pima County Fairgrounds
624-1013

San Xavier Pageant & Fiesta
*Commemorating the founding of
the mission, Tohono O'odham
and Yaqui cultures are featured.*
Mission San Xavier del Bac
622-6911

Spring Fling
*Annual carnival with food, rides
& games ushers in spring at the U.*
University of Arizona
621-5610

Tohono O'odham Arts Festival
*Native American arts & crafts on
display and for sale.*
Sells
602-383-2221

Tour of the Tucson Mountains (see p. 139)
*Bicycle race with 1,000
participants.*

745-2033
Tucson International Mariachi Conference
Amory Park & Tucson Convention Center (see p. 151)
770-7400
Tucson Toros AAA Baseball
Hi Corbett Field, Reid Park
791-4266
University of Arizona Baseball
Sancet Field
621-2411
Waila Festival
Tohono O'odham "chicken scratch" music, dance and food.
Arizona Historical Society
628-5774
Yaqui Easter Lenten Ceremonies
Mixture of Indian and Christian Observance of Easter
Old Pascua Village
785 W. Saguaro
791-4609

MAY
Casino Gambling
Las Vegas-style gambling hall on the Tohono O'odham reservation.
7350 S. Old Nogales Hwy
889-7354
Cinco de Mayo
Folk dancing, music, arts & crafts celebrating the Mexican victory over the French at Puebla in 1862.
Kennedy Park
623-8344
Greyhound Racing
Tucson Greyhound Park
2601 S. 3rd. Ave
884-7576
Jazz Sunday
Local and National musicians.
Reid Park
743-3399
Little Britches Rodeo
State championship for youngsters under 18.
Sierra Vista
602-458-3614
Southern Arizona Arabian Horse Ass'n Jubilee
Pima County Fairgrounds
624-1013
Tucson Toros AAA Baseball
Hi Corbett Field, Reid Park
791-4266
University of Arizona Baseball
Sancet Field
621-2411

JUNE
Casino Gambling
Las Vegas-style gambling hall on the Tohono O'odham reservation.
7350 S. Old Nogales Hwy
889-7354
Greyhound Racing
Tucson Greyhound Park
601 S. 3rd. Ave
884-7576
Juneteenth
Remembrance of the arrival of Union troops in Texas and of the Emancipation Proclamation.
Kennedy Park
791-4335
Music Festival
Mount Lemmon Ski Valley
576-1321
Tucson Toros AAA Baseball
Hi Corbett Field, Reid Park
791-4266
Shakespeare-in-the-Park
Reid Park
791-4079

JULY
4th of July Fireworks
Fireworks from "A" Mountain and several other location, check the paper.
Casino Gambling
Las Vegas-style gambling hall on the Tohono O'odham reservation.
7350 S. Old Nogales Hwy
889-7354
Greyhound Racing
Tucson Greyhound Park
2601 S. 3rd. Ave
884-7576
Herb Fair
Tucson Botanical Gardens
326-9255
Tucson Toros AAA Baseball
Hi Corbett Field, Reid Park
791-4266

AUGUST
Casino Gambling
Los Vegas-style gambling hall on the Tohono O'odham reservation.
7350 S. Old Nogales Hwy
889-7354
Fiesta de San Agustín
Fiesta honoring Tucson's patron saint.
Arizona Historical Society
628-5774
Greyhound Racing
Tucson Greyhound Park
2601 S. 3rd. Ave

884-7576
Tucson Toros AAA Baseball
    Hi Corbett Field, Reid Park
    791-4266
Vigilante Days
    Public hangings, shoot outs, food
    and dance.
    Tombstone
    602-457-2211

SEPTEMBER
Casino Gambling
    Las Vegas-style gambling hall
    on the Tohono O'odham
    reservation.
    7350 S. Old Nogales Hwy
    889-7354
Cochise County Fair
    Great cow country fair with
    horse racing.
    602-364-3819
Culinary Festival
    Top chefs from the state vie in
    cooking contest.
    Sheraton El Conquistador
    Resort 742-7000
Mexican Independence Day
    Folk dancing, music, food, arts
    & crafts
    Kennedy Park
    623-8344
Professional Tennis Tournament
    Randolph Tennis Center,
    Reid Park
    791-4896
Tucson Toros AAA Baseball
    Hi Corbett Field, Reid Park
    791-4266
University of Arizona Football
    Arizona Stadium
    621-2411

OCTOBER
Casino Gambling
    Las Vegas-style gambling hall
    on the Tohono O'odham
    reservation.
    7350 S. Old Nogales Hwy
    889-7354
Festival of Colors
    Hot air balloon festival.
    Sierra Vista
    602-458-6940
Fiesta de los Chiles
    Food, plants and art inspired by
    the fiery favorite.
    Tucson Botanical Gardens
    326-9255
Greyhound Racing
    Tucson Greyhound Park

2601 S. 3rd. Ave
884-7576
Helldorado Days
    Gun fights, Indian dancers,
    barbershop quartets, square
    dancing and food.
    Tombstone
    602-457-2211
Oktoberfest
    German bands, dancers and food.
    Mount Lemmon Ski Valley
    576-1321
Patagonia Fall Festival
    Arts, crafts entertainment and
    dance.
    Patagonia
    602-394-2387
Rex Allen Days
    A classic "local hero" celebration
    and the big event of the year in
    Willcox. Rodeo, fair, parade and
    Cowboy Hall of Fame induction.
    Willcox
    602-384-2272
University of Arizona Football
    Arizona Stadium
    621-2411

NOVEMBER
Casino Gambling
    Las Vegas-style gambling hall on
    the Tohono O'odham reservation.
    7350 S. Old Nogales Hwy
    889-7354
El Tour de Tucson (see p. 140)
    A big time bicycle race draws
    thousands of racers.
    Around the perimeter of Tucson.
    745-2033
Fort Lowell Arts & Crafts Fair
    Nice show in a pleasant setting.
    Fort Lowell Park
    791-4063
Greyhound Racing
    Tucson Greyhound Park
    2601 S. 3rd. Ave
    884-7576
Reid Park Arts & Crafts Show
    Usually great weather for a well
    attended show.
    Reid Park
    791-4063
Rillito Downs Quarter Horse Racing
    Parimutuel betting and a colorful
    atmosphere. (see p. 135)
    N.1st Ave. & Rillito River
    740-2690
Rugby Classic
    Major tournament draws

international players.
Hi Corbett Field, Reid Park
795-9949
Tucson Meet Yourself (see p. 150)
Food fest by community ethnic groups.
El Presidio Park
621-3392
University of Arizona Football
Arizona Stadium
621-2411
Western Music Festival Concerts
Showcase for top western musicians includes concerts and workshops.
Palo Verde Holiday Inn
323-3311

DECEMBER
4th Avenue Street Fair (see p. 147)
Huge selection of arts & crafts, food & street entertainers.
4th Avenue at University
624-5004
Balloon Glo (see p. 143)
Evening and morning show of hot air balloons on U of A campus.
University of Arizona
888-2954
Casino Gambling
Las Vegas-style gambling hall on the Tohono O'odham reservation.
7350 S. Old Nogales Hwy
889-7354
Copper Bowl Football Game
Major college teams battle it out each year.
Arizona Stadium
621-2411
Greyhound Racing
Tucson Greyhound Park
2601 S. 3rd. Ave
884-7576

Luminaria Nights
Traditional southwestern Christmas lights, music and refreshments.
Tucson Botanical Gardens
326-9255
Tumacacori Fiesta
Remembering the cultural heritage of the mission with food, entertainment and craft demonstrations.
Tumacacori National Monument
602-398-2704
Fiesta Navidad & Festival of Lights
Carolers and the traditional luminaries enliven this excellent Christmas shopping locale.
Tubac
602-398-9797
Rillito Downs Quarter Horse Racing
Parimutuel betting and a colorful atmosphere. (see p. 135)
N.1st Ave. & Rillito River
740-2690
University of Arizona Basketball
McKale Center
621-2411
University of Arizona Football
Arizona Stadium
621-2411
Winterhaven Festival of Lights
Fantastic neighborhood of homes decorated to the nines with Christmas lights and displays. Horse drawn wagons, walk or drive on designated evenings.
Winterhaven, Fort Lowell Rd. & Country Club Rd.

SUNRISE/SUNSET

	January	February	March	April
1st	7:25/5:30	7:17/5:57	6:51/6:21	6:12/6:43
5th	7:25/5:33	7:14/6:00	6:46/6:24	6:07/6:46
10th	7:25/5:37	7:10/6:05	6:40/6:28	6:02/6:48
15th	7:25/5:41	7:06/6:09	6:34/6:31	5:55/6:53
20th	7:23/5:46	7:01/6:13	6:27/6:35	5:49/6:56
25th	7:21/5:50	6:55/6:18	6:21/6:38	5:40/7:00
30th	7:10/5:55		6:14/6:42	5:39/7:03

	May	June	July	August
1st	5:38/7:04	5:18/7:25	5:21/7:34	5:39/7:21
5th	5:35/7:07	5:17/7:27	5:23/7:34	5:42/7:18
10th	5:30/7:10	5:17/7:29	5:25/7:33	5:45/7:13
15th	5:26/7:14	5:17/7:31	5:28/7:31	5:48/7:08
20th	5:23/7:17	5:18/7:33	5:31/7:29	5:51/7:03
25th	5:21/7:21	5:19/7:34	5:34/7:26	5:55/6:57
30th	5:19/7:24	5:21/7:34	5:38/7:23	5:58/6:51

	September	October	November	December
1st	5:59/6:49	6:18/6:10	6:41/5:35	7:07/5:19
5th	6:01/6:44	6:20/6:05	6:44/5:31	7:10/5:19
10th	6:05/6:37	6:24/5:58	6:48/5:28	7:14/5:19
15th	6:08/6:31	6:27/5:52	6:53/5:24	7:17/5:21
20th	6:11/6:24	6:31/5:47	6:57/5:22	7:20/5:23
25th	6:14/6:17	6:35/5:41	7:02/5:20	7:22/5:25
30th	6:17/6:11	6:39/5:36	7:06/5:19	7:24/5:28

NOTE: First times denotes sunrise, second time denotes sunset.
©Compiled from U.S. Weather Service Data

TEMPERATURE

	TUCSON AIRPORT HIGH	RANGER STATION HIGH	TUCSON AIRPORT LOW	RANGER STATION LOW
JANUARY	64°	44°	37°	25°
FEBRUARY	67°	45°	38°	25°
MARCH	73°	49°	44°	27°
APRIL	82°	57°	49°	33°
MAY	92°	68°	57°	41°
JUNE	98°	74°	68°	48°
JULY	97°	75°	72°	52°
AUGUST	96°	73°	71°	50°
SEPTEMBER	94°	68°	65°	45°
OCTOBER	85°	59°	55°	37°
NOVEMBER	74°	52°	45°	30°
DECEMBER	67°	45°	39°	23°

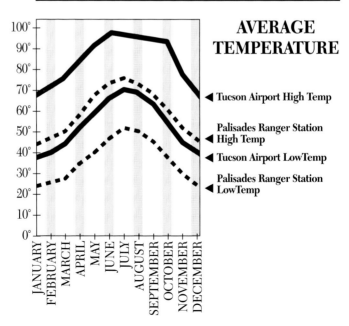

AVERAGE TEMPERATURE

◀ Tucson Airport High Temp

◀ Palisades Ranger Station High Temp

◀ Tucson Airport Low Temp

◀ Palisades Ranger Station Low Temp

RAIN FALL

AVERAGE RAIN FALL

JANUARY	0.83
FEBRUARY	0.75
MARCH	0.74
APRIL	0.45
MAY	0.14
JUNE	0.2
JULY	2.09
AUGUST	2.06
SEPTEMBER	1.15
OCTOBER	0.61
NOVEMBER	0.6
DECEMBER	1.11

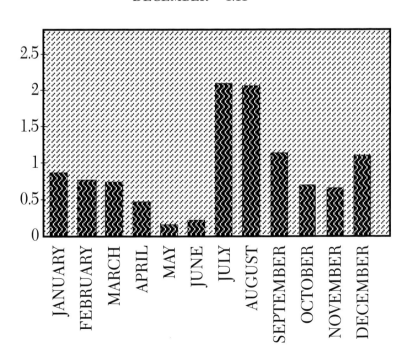

WILDFLOWERS

FLOWERING DESERT PLANTS	PEAK BLOOMING
Ajo lily Hesperocallis undulata	Last Half of March
Arizona poppy Kallstroemia grandiflora	First Half of August
Asters Aster spp.	First Half of September
Barrel cactus or **Bisnaga Ferocactus** spp.	First Half of August
Bear grass Nolina microcarpa	First Half of June
Beaver tail Opuntia basilaris	Last Half of April
Bladderpod mustard Lesquerella gordoni	Last Half of February
Brittle bush Encelia farinosa	Last Half of March
Buffalo gourd Cucurbita foetidissima	Last Half of July
Canaigre Rumex hymenosepalus	First Half of March
Chaenactis Chaenactis fremontii	Last Half of March
Cholla Opuntia spp.	First Half of May
Christmas cactus Opuntia leptocaulis	Last Half of June
Coral bean Erythrina flabelliformis	Last Half of May
Covena or **Desert hyacinth** Brodlaea pulchella	First Half of March
Creosote bush Larrea ridentata	First Half of April
Desert broom Baccharis sarothroides	September -February
Desert chicory Rafinesquia neomexicana	Last Half of March
Desert daisy Melampodium leucanthum	Last Half of March
Desert dandelion Malcothrix glabrata	Last half of March
Desert mallow Sphaeralcea spp.	Last Half of March
Desert marigold Baileya multiradiata	First Half of April
Desert senna Cassia covesii	Last Half of May
Desert star Monoptilon bellioides	Last Half of March
Desert willow Chilopsis linearis	First Half of May
Devilsclaw Proboscidea spp.	First Half of Aug.
Evening primrose Oenothera spp.	First Half of February.
Fairy duster Calliandra eriophylla	Last Half of March
Fleabane Erigeron divergens	First Half of November
Fiddle neck Amsinckia intermedia	Last Half of March
Filaree Erodium circutarium	First Half of April
Fishhook cactus Mammillaria spp.	Last Half of July
Gilias Gills spp.	Last Half of March
Goldfields Baeria chrysostoma	Last Half of March

FLOWERING DESERT PLANTS	PEAK BLOOMING
Hedgehog cactus Echinocereus spp.	Last Half of April
Indian wheat Plantago purshii	Last Half of March
Ironweed Olneya testate	Last Half of May
Jimson weed Datura meteloides	Last Half of July
Joshua tree Yucca brevifolia	Last Half of March
Jumping cholla Opuntia fulgida	Last Half of July
Loco weed Astraglalus spp.	First Half of March
Lupine Lupinus sparsiflorus and others	Last Half of March
Mariposa lily (*orange*) Calochortus kennedvi	Last Half of April
Mesquite Prosopis velutina	Last Half of April
Monkey flower Mimulus spp.	Last Half of March
Night blooming cereus Peniocereus greggii	Last Half of June
Ocotillo Fouquieria splendens	Last Half of April
Old man cactus Lophocereus schotkii	Last Half of May
Organ pipe cactus Lemaireocereus thurberi	Last Half of May
Owl clover Orthocarpus purpurascens	Last Half of March
Paloverde (*blue*) Carcidium floridum	Last Half of April
Paloverde (*foothill*) Carcidium microphyllum	First Half of May
Paper flower Psilostrophe cooperi	First Half of May
Penstemon Penstemon barbatus	Last Half of May
Penstemon Penstemon parryi	First Half of March
Phacelias Phacelia spp.	Last Half of March
Poppy (*golden or Calif.*) Eschscholtzia mexicana	Last Half of March
Prickly pears (*common*) Opuntia spp.	First Half of May
Rabbit brush Chrysothamnus spp.	Last Half of October
Saguaro Carnegeia gigantea	First Half of June
Sand verbena Abronia villosa	First Half of March
Sandwash senecio Senecio douglasii	First Half of March
Soaptree yucca Yucca elate	Mid-June
Sotol Dasylirion wheeleri	Last Half of June
Squawberry Lycium pallidum	First Half of May
Tackstem Calycoseris wrightii	Last Half of March
Teddy bear cactus Opuntia bigelovii	Last Half of May
Verbena Verbena spp.	Last Half of March
Whitehorn Acacia constricta	Last Half of May
Wild onion Aliium macropetalum	First Half of March
Yucca (*broadleaf*) Yucca baccata	Last Half of March
Yucca (broadleaf) Yucca schidigera	Last Half of March

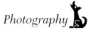

PHOTO BASICS

The **Tools.** If you stick to the major brands, you will usually get equipment which will render fine images. If this is an important hobby to you, get a 35mm camera with interchangeable lenses. Most have autofocus and autoexposure which can be overridden by the user. Zoom lenses are much better than they used to be, and will allow great flexibility. There is a bewildering variety of equipment available.

The best ways to make purchase decisions are to trust the salesperson at a reputable camera store or educate yourself by reading reading *Shutterbug* and *Popular Photography* magazines for several months. Most people probable do some of both.

If you have access to a computer with a modem, I highly recommend logging onto **Compuserve** and accessing the Photoforum to ask questions of experiencecd photographers. If you are shy about asking questions or don't know what to ask, just browsing through the message section will be a real education in current photography technology.

Film. Kodak and Fuji both make great films. Avoid the faster films for scenics unless there is a particular reason to use them. Fuji's Velvia 50 ISO and Kodak Elite 100 ISO are often used by pros shooting for magazines. Most shoot the Fuji at 40 ISO to avoid dark images.

Unless you hope to sell your images or project them in slide shows, you probably should stick to print film. You are more likely to get a well-exposed print from print film than having a print made from a slide. There are several choices and either Kodak Gold 100 or Fujicolor 100 are hard to beat. Avoid one-hour processing unless you are familiar with the place. There is a tendency to overuse chemistry to save money and this can ruin or degrade your treasured images.

Composition. What follows is only a smattering of common "rules of thumb" used by many experienced photographers. Once you understand them you are free to break them. If you are committed to becoming a better photographer, take a course at a local school or photo shop. There are many good books on the subject as well. I can recommend:

The Joy of Photography; Eastman Kodak
Basic Techniques of Photography, An Ansel Adams Guide; John P. Schafer
Mountain Light; Galen Rowell

Very Basics

1. Shot with the sun coming over your shoulder or from the side; shooting into the sun will often wash out images.
2. Get close enough to the subject, generally fill the viewfinder.
3. Don't put the subject square in the middle of the frame, place

it slightly off to the side or up or down by 1/3. Study the "rule of thirds" in one of the recommended books.

4. Use a tripod or brace the camera to prevent blurry pictures when the shutter speed is less then the focal length of the lenses. i.e., if the zoom lenses setting is 100mm the shutter speed usually must be 1/100th of a second or higher to get a sharp image.

5. If using a small flash built into the camera, shoot from within 10-15 feet of the subject. These small units will not illuminate the scene much beyond that distance, perhaps a little farther if you are using fast film.

People. Pros use "portrait" lenses, usually 80 to 100 mm. A zoom set at these lengths works as well. Get close as a general rule. If you are shooting "candid" shots where the subject is not posing, shoot a lot of film, many frames will not come out. Use flash in bright outdoor settings to get the shadows out of people's faces, especially from hats. For parties and the like, use a wide-angle lenses to get everyone in the picture. Again, a zoom like a 28 to 80 mm fits the bill very well.

Scenics.. Avoid shooting in midday, the best shots will be in the hour or two after sunrise and before sunset. For sunrise and sunset you will need a tripod because of the slow shutter speeds required by the low light. Wide desert and mountain vistas that awe your eye will sometimes make boring images. Try putting an interesting subject in the foreground for scale. Usually wide lenses are best for scenics but long lenses can also produce interesting results to "stack" features or catch the effect of light on a subject across a canyon. Flash sometimes can be used effectively in scenics to illuminate a back lit subject.

Action. ISO 100 speed film will usually be fast enough unless you are using a very long and slow lense. Capturing an action image in "freeze frame" is not always the most interesting technique. To express the dynamics of an action scene try one of the following ideas.

"Panning" is a technique in which you hold the camera on the subject as it moves and press the shutter while the camera is still moving. The subject will be frozen but the background will be blurred. This is the easiest method because you do not have to change any camera settings and it can be done with even the simplest camera.

Trickier, but sometimes very effective is using a slow shutter speed, if your camera is adjustable. If your camera has a shutter priority mode set the shutter for 1/30th or less. If it only has an aperture priority mode chose a small aperture which will cause the camera to select a slow shutter speed. Hold the camera stationary and steady as the subject moves by and you will get a blurred image which conveys motion of the subject with the background relatively visible but perhaps a little blurred from the low shutter speed if you hand held the camera. If you elect to experiment with this method be sure take some shots with a higher shutter speed (at least 1/125) to freeze the action so you have some acceptable images recording the event to take home.

NIGHT PHOTOGRAPHY

Many automatic cameras can take pictures of bright night scenes. Just use a tripod and a shutter release. If your camera cannot, or if you want to experiment, choose the manual settings from the Exposure Value Table, using the suggestions on the lower left. The EV Table is for ISO 100 film. Add 1 to suggested values if you're using ISO 200 and add 2 for ISO 400, etc.

SHUTTER SPEED

EV	1/8000	1/4000	1/2000	1/1000	1/500	1/250	1/125	1/60	1/30	1/15	1/8	1/4	1/2	1"	2"	4"	8"	15"	30"	1'	2'	4'	8'	16'	32'	64'
-8																						1	1.4	2	2.8	4
-7																					1	1.4	2	2.8	4	5.6
-6																				1	1.4	2	2.8	4	5.6	8
-5																			1	1.4	2	2.8	4	5.6	8	11
-4																		1	1.4	2	2.8	4	5.6	8	11	16
-3																	1	1.4	2	2.8	4	5.6	8	11	16	22
-2																1	1.4	2	2.8	4	5.6	8	11	16	22	32
-1															1	1.4	2	2.8	4	5.6	8	11	16	22	32	45
0														1	1.4	2	2.8	4	5.6	8	11	16	22	32	45	64
1													1	1.4	2	2.8	4	5.6	8	11	16	22	32	45	64	
2												1	1.4	2	2.8	4	5.6	8	11	16	22	32	45	64		
3											1	1.4	2	2.8	4	5.6	8	11	16	22	32	45	64			
4										1	1.4	2	2.8	4	5.6	8	11	16	22	32	45	64				
5									1	1.4	2	2.8	4	5.6	8	11	16	22	32	45	64					
6								1	1.4	2	2.8	4	5.6	8	11	16	22	32	45	64						
7							1	1.4	2	2.8	4	5.6	8	11	16	22	32	45	64							
8						1	1.4	2	2.8	4	5.6	8	11	16	22	32	45	64								
9					1	1.4	2	2.8	4	5.6	8	11	16	22	32	45	64									
10				1	1.4	2	2.8	4	5.6	8	11	16	22	32	45	64										
11			1	1.4	2	2.8	4	5.6	8	11	16	22	32	45	64											
12		1	1.4	2	2.8	4	5.6	8	11	16	22	32	45	64												
13	1	1.4	2	2.8	4	5.6	8	11	16	22	32	45	64													
14	1.4	2	2.8	4	5.6	8	11	16	22	32	45	64														
15	2	2.8	4	5.6	8	11	16	22	32	45	64															
16	2.8	4	5.6	8	11	16	22	32	45	64																
17	4	5.6	8	11	16	22	32	45	64																	
18	5.6	8	11	16	22	32	45	64																		
19	8	11	16	22	32	45	64																			
20	11	16	22	32	45	64																				
21	16	22	32	45	64																					
22	22	32	45	64																						
23	32	45	64																							
24	45	64																								
25	64																									

APERTURE

Subject Matter	EV
Cityscape at night	1
Cityscape immediately after sunset	10
Cityscape at twilight	8
Bright city lights	7
Fireworks	9
Landscape by moonlight	-3
Full moon itself	14
Floodlite sports	8
Floodlite buildings	4
Lightning - Set shutter to "B" and hold it open with a shutter release until one or more strikes are recorded. WARNING. This is dangerous, you can be struck up to five miles from the storm.	

The following is a very short list of the best information available about the Tucson area. It is strongly suggested that you spend time browsing at one of the many fine book stores in Tucson to find material that suits your needs and tastes. The best places to get topographic maps are Tucson Map & Flag Center, 3239 N. 1st Ave. and the Summit Hut, 5045 E. Speedway Blvd.

Periodicals

Desert Skies; quarterly magazine published by the Summit Hut, excellent outdoor information.

Tucson Guide; quarterly magazine with restaurant guide and good features on area attractions.

Tucson Weekly; full coverage of the local entertainment scene.

Arizona Daily Star; local newspaper has excellent features on area attractions.

Tucson Citizen; local newspaper has excellent features on area attractions.

Maps

Arizona Road Map; Arizona Highways (good basic resource)

Arizona Road Atlas; Arizona Highways (recommended)

U.S. Forest Service Maps of Coronado National Forest (excellent)

Nature Guides

Cactus of the Southwest; W. Hubert Earle

Deserts; The Audubon Society Nature Guides

Deserts of the Southwest; Peggy Larson

Field Guide to Western Birds; Roger Tory Peterson

Flowers of the Southwest Deserts; Natt N. Dodge

Flowers of the Southwest Mountains; Leslie P. Arnberger

Shrubs & Tress of the Southwest Uplands; Francis H. Elmore

Venomous Animals of Arizona; Robert L. Smith

Hiking Guides

Tucson Hiking Guide; Betty Leavengood (good chatty guide which covers a selection of popular hikes around the Tucson Area)

Catalina Hiking Guide; Cowgill & Glendening (the complete hiking guide to the Catalinas, a little dated)

Southern Arizona Hiking Club Maps of the Catalinas, Rincons and Santa Ritas (indispensable for serious hikers)

Rockclimbing Guides

Squeezing the Lemmon; A Rock Climbers Guide to the Mt. Lemmon Highway; Eric Fazio-Rhicard

Backcountry Rockclimbing in Southern Arizona; Bob Kerry

Nature Photography Books and Magazines

Basic Guide to Close-up Photography; H.P. Book

Close-up Photography; Kodak Workshop Series

Existing Light Photography; Kodak Workshop Series

Guide to 35mm Photography; Kodak Book

How to Photograph Flowers, Plants & Landscapes; H.P. Book

How to Take Great Nature & Wildlife Photos; H.P. Book

Claude Nuridsany & Marie Perennou, Photographing Nature, Oxford University Press, 1976. (Close-up & macro photography)*

SLR Photographer's Handbook; H.P. Book (Author; Carl Shipman, three of the photographers: Jack Dykinga, Thomas Wiewandt & C. Allen Morgan, all Tucsonans)*

*Outdoor Photographer (Magazine)**
**Particularly recommended*

Back Roads

Ghost Towns of Arizona; James & Barbara Sherman (good maps, direc tions and historic photos)

Backroads of Arizona; Earl Thollander (fine drawings and a personal, inspiring text)

History

American Indians of the Southwest; Bertha P. Dutton (an overview of the diversity of Native Americans in the Southwest)

Life Among the Apaches; John C. Cremony (a comtemporary account of the conflict between the Apaches and the Americans, highly recom mended)

Tucson: A Short History; Southwestern Mission Research Center (con cise view of Tucson's History)

Hispanic Arizona, 1536-1856; James E. Officer (fine scholarly work, recommended)

Los Tucsonenses; The Mexican Community if Tucson, 1854-1941 (per sonal family accounts highlight this interesting work)

Arizona Place Names; Will C. Barnes (a classic resource for understand ing Arizona)

INDEX